The HUMAN TOUCH

The
HUMAN TOUCH

PAUL H. DUNN

Bookcraft
Salt Lake City, Utah

Library of Congress Catalog Card Number: 83-62419
ISBN O-88494-502-2

5 6 7 8 9 10   89 88 87 86 85 84

Lithographed in the United States of America
PUBLISHERS PRESS
Salt Lake City, Utah

Preface

Jesus Christ was and is the Son of God and Savior of the world. He is divine. He also had a mortal mother and through his unique heritage could comprehend both the divine and the human. While always teaching his listeners the divine nature, he never lost the "human touch."

Over the years I have tried to emulate the Master. He has been my Lord and Teacher. I have tried to apply his techniques of using stories and examples in conveying gospel principles. As the Savior taught, his use of words always brought to our minds picture after picture and we see his genius in touching the human soul.

This volume is another attempt on the part of the author to "teach correct principles" through life experiences and examples. Individuals still struggle and seek solutions to daily challenges. *The Human Touch* is a book that hopefully will give the reader additional insight and strength in overcoming his concerns.

This book is not endorsed by The Church of Jesus Christ of Latter-day Saints and I alone am fully responsible for its contents. I hereby absolve the Church and its leaders from any responsibility for error this volume may contain.

I am grateful to many for this publication. I express particular thanks and appreciation to my daughter Janet Gough for her editorial assistance and marvelous insights. Many of her suggestions are included. I am grateful to my able secretary, Colleen Erickson, for typing the manuscript and the many hours in proofreading and checking sources. Special thanks to David Christensen, my friend, for insights and ideas.

As always, I am most grateful to my wife, Jeanne, and daughters, Janet, Marsha, and Kellie for continued support and encouragement. My special appreciation to Bookcraft for our long association and relationship.

Contents

Part I / Your Self

Part II / Those Close

Part III / Your World

Part IV / Your Values

I
Your Self

The Power To Change

The older I get, the more I realize the importance of certain things and the un-importance of others. Some things matter; some don't. I am also beginning to understand more than ever before the vital, life-or-death implications of two or three principles in particular. I have thought about these a good deal. The following are clues alluding to one well-known human characteristic. What would be your answer to this riddle?

"I am your constant companion.

"I am your greatest helper, or your heaviest burden.

"I will push you onward or drag you down to failure.

"I am completely at your command.

"Half the tasks you do you might just as well turn over to me and I will be able to do them quickly and correctly.

"I am easily managed, you must merely be firm with me.

"Show me exactly how you want something done, and after a few lessons I will do it automatically.

"I am the servant of all great men and also, of all failures as well.

"Those who are great—I have made failures.

"I am not a machine, but I work with all the precision of a machine, plus the intelligence of a man.

"You may run me for profit or run me for ruin—it makes no difference to me.

"Take me, train me, be firm with me and I will put the world at your feet.

"Be easy with me and I will destroy you."

(From Daryl Hoole, *The Joys of Homemaking*, p. 9.)

Do you have it yet? You probably are well acquainted with this powerful fellow. He is a part of you. In his own words: "I am habit!"

I get a kick out of people who say they have no habits. We *all* have habits. Breathing is a habit. Sleeping is a habit; so are eating, walking, and talking. The trick is to have *good* habits and eliminate the *bad*. Mahatma Gandhi put it in a few words. He said, "Man's destined purpose is to conquer all habits, to overcome the evil in him and to restore good to its rightful place."

Now, did you notice the word Gandhi used? He said "restore" good to its rightful place. If we *restore* something, we *return* it to its original place. May I suggest, therefore, that we are all basically good—at least, we once were. After all, we lived with heavenly parents before this life. Our task is to prepare ourselves to go back home. You may be familiar with these lyrics sung by children the world over:

> I am a child of God
> And he has sent me here,

Has given me an earthly home
With parents kind and dear.

Lead me, guide me, walk beside me,
Help me find the way.
Teach me all that I must do
To live with him someday.
("I Am a Child of God," *Sing with Me*, B-76.)

Well, the Lord teaches us to get busy replacing our bad habits with good; to make progress in our struggle with self. After all, it's going to take a while. One way or another, our habits are going to have an eternal impact, just as they do right now. It was James, the apostle, who said, "A double minded man is unstable in all his ways" (James 1:8).

The more we overcome our bad habits and replace them with good, the more stable we'll become. Our words and actions will begin to match as never before. The question is, how do we keep our good habits while eliminating the bad? As always, the Lord has given us the answer. Here is what he says:

"For the power is in them, wherein they are agents unto themselves. And inasmuch as men do good they shall in nowise lose their reward." (D&C 58:28.)

We may not like the answer, but there it is. The power is within each one of us. It's up to us! I know that a kind Heavenly Father will help us, and that without his help we won't make it, but it's still up to us. He can't do it for us. *We* must begin the process of change.

May I suggest that the first step is a very simple one: We have to face the fact that we *do* have a habit that needs to be changed, and then with a desire to do something about it, we must start.

But even recognizing that we have a problem isn't always easy. I once heard of a man by the name of

Wilson who slept so much that his friends called him Rip Van Wilson. Refusing to face his bad habit he simply replied, "I don't sleep long, I just sleep slow."

Then there are those who say they know they have a problem; they really *would* like to overcome it, but they just can't. In fact, such an incident recently came to my attention.

"A concerned mother pleaded with her son to stop smoking, and his only reply was, 'I can't. It has gotten to be a habit with me.'

"Early the following morning the son was awakened by a stinging willow striking his feet. He was so startled at what his mother was doing that he didn't ask for an explanation. This happened again the next morning, and the next, and finally the boy asked, 'Mother, what has gotten into you? Why are you hitting me?'

"The mother answered, 'I don't know. See, I have this habit and I can't quit.'" (Dorothy Winder, "Things They're Saying," *The New Era*, February 1974, p. 19.)

We can guess what happened. There's not one of us who can't overcome habits if we decide we want to and *he* gives us help. But either one of those steps left out won't do it. We must do *our* part and the Lord will do *his*. A young lady observed that very principle in action in her own home not long ago. Here are her insightful words:

"My mother was telling me and two of my aunts about my father who prayed for help and had successfully overcome a bad habit. 'Hmm,' I mused, 'maybe I ought to pray for help to lose ten pounds.' An aunt observed, 'Maybe it would be better to fast and pray.'" (Janet Houston, *Ensign*.)

You see what I mean? They go together!

We all know that overcoming bad habits is a battle. I am reminded of a couplet I learned as a young boy:

Bad habits gather in unseen degrees,
As brooks run to rivers and rivers run to seas.

It makes no difference what the habit is: eating too much, smoking, drinking, drugs, foul language, immorality, lying, procrastinating, or whatever. Some are small habits; some large. The principle to remember is that they can all be overcome and the process is the same. There are occasions when professional help is needed and appropriate. But even then, *we* must do the changing—and we can!

If you should walk into the office of a colleague of mine, you will see this motto posted plainly for all to see: "You cannot run away from a weakness, you must sometime fight it out or perish; and if that be so, why not now?" (Robert Louis Stevenson.) That's the question: Why not *now*?

I promise you that all evil *can* be overcome. Bad habits *can* be replaced with good. Change *can* take place in all of us. Together with the Lord's help we *can* regain his presence. Now is the time for us to make that commitment. Decide what we want to change, but realize that we won't overcome everything at once. It will take time. Hence the need to begin now.

Satan will try to discourage us. He will do all he can to stop us, but we have within us the power to conquer the adversary.

With that commitment, may we receive assurance that the words of John are true: "He that overcometh shall inherit all things; and I will be his God, and he shall be my son." (Revelation 21:7.)

It is my witness that one of the greatest blessings in life is to retire to our bed at night with a clear conscience, knowing that although we have a long way to go, we are honestly trying to overcome.

Conquering Self

I have appreciated several quotes which, over the years, have had great influence on my life. The first is from Thomas O'Shaughnessy:

"No man can be free until he conquers himself. Many mistake slavery for liberty; they think liberty consists in following their desires, passions...[but] mistaking the mere license of passion or of sensual appetite for liberty binds [them] in a stern bondage.... The price of freedom is mastery over passion and ignorance...the only road to liberty is through obedience;...man can control nature only while he obeys God's laws [and] must master the forces within ...and the conditions without...every individual must first obtain victory over self, for selfishness is the cause of all slavery." (Thomas O'Shaughnessy, "Liberty and Freedom," *Overland Monthly,* September 1918.)

The second comes from Winthrop W. Aldrich: "It must be the aim of education to teach the citizen that he must first of all rule himself."

The third is by John Locke: "Every man must sometime or other be trusted to himself."

Fourth, the Lord has said:

"Enter ye in at the strait gate: for wide is the gate, and broad is the way, that leadeth to destruction, and many there be which go in thereat:

"Because strait is the gate, and narrow is the way, which leadeth unto life, and few there be that find it." (Matthew 7:13-14.)

"If ye know these things, happy are ye if ye do them." (John 13:17.)

If we really want to be happy now *and* in eternity, we must come to the point that we can conquer ourselves. Self-discipline is a key to all that is good and worthwhile. The gate is straight and the way is narrow. But it is not *too* straight and it is not *too* narrow.

The blessing of self-control does not come easily. I am reminded of a story shared by Bertrand F. Harrison about a young boy who learned, as we all do, by experience:

"This would be the best-looking racing car on the block—Dale was sure of it. He had been working on it for two weeks now and it was all but finished. Just a couple more strips of tin for the cowling would make it ready for the first try-out. He swung vigorously to drive a nail through the metal; the hammer came down hard, but on the wrong nail—the nail of Dale's left thumb. A shriek of pain resounded throughout the garage workshop as Dale hurled the hammer with all of his might to the end of the garage. The handle flipped over, smashing one of the windows. Bits of glass came tinkling down on the concrete floor. Dale did not make a habit of swearing, but the events of the past half-hour had been just too much for almost anybody, and he let go with a couple of expressions that do not appear in the dictionary.

"From his chair on the back porch Mr. Stevens had watched with interest as his son put the finishing touches on his racing car. As the hammer went flying against the end of the garage, he chuckled to himself, remembering a not-too-different occasion in his own boyhood. Clearly this outburst demanded some action, but he waited a few minutes before he went to the door and called: 'Dale, would you like to go for a little ride with me?'

"Dale was not in the mood to do any more on the racing car, but then he was not so keen on going for a ride either. Still, he had a suspicion the hammer incident had not gone unnoticed, so he thought it best to go along without argument.

"Traveling south, Dale and his father were soon out of town. A few miles west and then south again and they were near the northeast corner of the farm where Mr. Stevens had lived as a boy. The car was parked along the roadside and father and son climbed to the top of a small rocky knoll. Pointing to two boulders placed one at each end of a low mound Mr. Stevens asked: 'Do you see those rocks?'

" 'Yes,' Dale replied, 'it looks like a grave.'

" 'It is a grave—this is where we buried old Nibs, the best horse we ever owned. One day your grandpa was pulling out a tree stump; and as it came free from the hole, it gave a crazy twist, flipped over and knocked grandpa down right in front of the advancing stump. He was in a pretty dangerous spot, but he yelled for old Nibs to "Whoa!" Old Nibs stopped on the spot and stood still till grandpa could free himself. Farm work can often be dangerous. Several times someone got in a tight spot, but you could always depend on old Nibs to stop when you told him to or to go when you wanted him to go. He was always under complete control. It was a sad day in our family when he died. That's why we buried him here and marked his grave with stones.' " (Bertrand F. Harrison, "The Strength That Makes Us Free," *Instructor,* July 1960, p. 240.)

Well, the point was made and a young man began to understand the great principles of self-discipline.

Another young person, a young woman, who recounts her struggle with self-control gives her key to success. Like many of us, her greatest desire was to turn her dreams into reality. She knew it would be difficult but she finally came to the point she was determined to give it her best try. She says:

"First I decided to tackle the everyday things I should be doing. I started to read at least an hour every day in the Bible or Book of Mormon. Then I made myself pray every day *on my knees.* (I used to just say my prayers in bed, too lazy to get on my knees.) Then I made myself clean my room every day—keep it spic and span. My mom couldn't believe it when she realized I was serious about my goals.

"When I found I could succeed, I just kept going. I couldn't stand to get up in the morning, let alone go outside in the cold and run around, so I prayed that I would be able to jog and lose some weight and get back into shape. I made myself get up an hour earlier than usual and go outside and jog every morning in the dark and cold. Then I'd take a shower, fix a good breakfast, get ready for work, study the scriptures, and leave. I'm sure it was the Lord who gave me the strength to do what was necessary to reach this goal.

"How do you learn to master yourself? I found that you start by doing the little things so you can move on to bigger and better things. You work hard to be consistent. And most important, you ask for the Lord's help." (Susan Munson, "Dreams," *The New Era,* December 1981, p. 26.)

With that kind of determination, imagine the kind of person we could each become.

I mentioned Susan as she gives us an important key to the conquest of self. If determination alone would do it there would be many more of us who would have a high degree of self-control. But determination alone will not always do it. It often takes a greater power than our own. In Susan's own words, "ask for the Lord's help." That seems overly simple, perhaps, but it works. It certainly beats the statement a certain young man made: "I'm going to overcome my procrastination ... first thing in the morning." For most of us that "morning" never comes. At least it doesn't without some real help from our Heavenly Father. He is available. He is willing and anxious to help, but requires of us to ask and seek. He desires our happiness now and our return to his presence later on. But these goals cannot be obtained without self-discipline.

It would be interesting to know the ages of those who have read this chapter. How many are under twenty-one? twenty-one to thirty? over thirty? over fifty? over seventy? over ninety? The reason I ask is that I wonder how many doubt their ability to learn self-control as a result of age. I find it amazing that those who have smoked all their lives can stop in one day when told by a doctor that they must quit or else. Motivation is a wonderful thing. I have seen men and women in their eighties and nineties make major changes in their lives when the cause was right. Imagine what could happen if we all prayed sincerely and constantly for the strength to discipline ourselves. What a difference that would make in our own lives as well as in the lives of our family and friends! The struggle would be worth it. An author I have not been able to identify talked about that struggle. He said:

"The greatest battle of life is fought out within the silent chambers of the soul. A victory on the inside of a man's heart is worth a hundred conquests on the battlefields of life. To be master of yourself is the best guarantee that you will be master of the situation. Know thyself. The crown of character is self-control." (Quoted in Spencer W. Kimball, *The Miracle of Forgiveness*, Bookcraft, 1969, p. 235.)

I have been involved in the sports world since I was a young man. I love athletics and the lessons that can be learned through participation in them. There is something special about the thrill of victory, and there is even a special feeling in the agony of defeat. Win or lose, there is a special "something" when an athlete brings into his life the discipline necessary to excel. That excellence is often measured not against others but against himself. But I know of little else quite as sad, in or out of the sports world, as someone who exclaims: "If only...!" And then the phrase varies with the individual. "If only I hadn't said that." "If only I hadn't got started." "If only I could change what happened." Or, as was said so poignantly in the movie *West Side Story:* "I wish it was yesterday."

Let me reassure us all that such phrases need not be repeated. You and I can control our own destiny. The Lord will help us. I know he will. As the poet Longfellow penned:

The heights by great men reached and kept
Were not attained by sudden flight,
But they, while their companions slept,
Were toiling upward in the night.

We can do it! The toil is worth it! Husbands, your wives will appreciate the difference. Wives, your husbands will enjoy the changes. Children, your parents will be pleasantly shocked with the difference. Parents, your children will love you for your strength.

May we all think seriously about our own self-control. And, with the help of God's power, may we begin a quest that will change our lives now and forever.

Be Yourself

Have you ever noticed that babies aren't born with inferiority complexes? During those first few weeks and months of life there's nobody they love better than themselves. They fairly sparkle with self-approval. Show a baby his face in the mirror and he's entranced for minutes, oohing and aahing at how wonderful he is.

Do you feel that same way about looking at your face in the mirror? Most of us don't. We may not be born with inferiority complexes, but it doesn't take long for all of us on earth to develop some. As a wise man once said, "To be human is to feel inferior." No matter how confident or good-looking or talented another person appears to be, he has his pockets of inferiority just as you do.

The reason for this is simple. Will Rogers said it. "We're all ignorant, only about different things." We are all inferior in some areas. Not any one of us is *the* best looking, best built, cleverest, wittiest, most athletic, funniest, kindest person on earth. You're bound to find someone who tops you in one way or another wherever you go.

A young homemaker I knew went visiting in her neighborhood one afternoon. At her first stop she visited a friend who was just redecorating her living room. The room was being done with immaculate taste. And the young homemaker thought, "I can't decorate like this."

At her second stop she met a neighbor who painted landscapes and portraits. Some of the neighbor's work had won prizes. She had had her own showings in the city's private art galleries. And the young homemaker thought, "I can't paint like that."

At her third stop she talked to a neighbor who was preparing lunch for a dozen of the neighborhood kids. It seems children from up and down the block flocked to her home every day just to be near her. And the young homemaker thought, "Children don't like me like that."

By the time she went home, the young woman was totally depressed and felt like a no-account. But, you know, that same kind of experience happens to each of us every day. We are frankly surrounded by people who are better at lots of things than we are. The person with a happy, healthy attitude toward his life is the one who wholeheartedly accepts that none of us can do everything well. He can admire the strengths and abilities of another without feeling envious or put down. He accepts himself for who he is and relishes his own strengths.

A particularly well-adjusted friend of mine said this about another superbly talented man we know. "Well," he said, "if I could do everything he could, then he wouldn't be unique anymore."

Anyone who spends much time observing the earth must be impressed with the Lord's love of making unique things; no two sunsets or two snow-flakes are the same. As science has noted, except for identical twins, the odds against two individuals being born exactly alike are astronomical. There are more than eight million ways the twenty-three chromosomes of a human mother and the twenty-three of a father can combine. The odds against any two of their children having the same complement of chromosomes are about seventy trillion to one. And since each chromosome may have 1,240 genes, the odds against two identical individuals reach a number so high, it doesn't even have a name; it would have to be written as 1 followed by 9,032 zeros.

The point is, you're not like anybody else. You're one of a kind. You cannot be someone else. You were never meant to be. You are inferior to your comrades in a hundred ways, but there are just as many ways they are inferior to you. You can never begin to plumb the strengths that are uniquely yours until you can accept yourself for who you are. As long as you are trying to be someone else, you'll always be aching and miserable.

Ralph Waldo Emerson, the great genius of American letters, said this in his essay on "Self-Reliance," "There is a time in every man's education when he arrives at the conviction that envy is igno-rance; that imitation is suicide; that he must take him-self for better for worse as his portion; that though the wide universe is full of good, no kernel of nourishing corn can come to him but through his toil bestowed on that plot of ground which is given to him to till. ... The power which resides in him is new in nature, and none but he knows what that is which he can do, nor does he know until he has tried."

Emerson said, "Trust thyself." We cannot conduct our lives always looking over our shoulder to see what our neighbor can do. We must find out what we can do, what our gleam of life is, where our star leads. Our neighbor cannot confirm or deny our path. It is not his.

So, when you have twinges of inferiority, remember that your neighbor's strengths or weaknesses have nothing to do with you. Your task is simply to accept yourself and become what you must be. Throughout man's history, we have always valued the unique, not the mass-produced. Every year, thousands of tourists visit Pisa to see its famous leaning tower. The tower leans more than sixteen feet out of the perpendicular as if to defy gravity and the demands of architectural tradition. We value it because it is one of a kind—because it seems to insist on being what it is and nothing else. On the seashore we value the shell that is unique, that is set apart from the others, that dares to be what it is.

And each of us must first be true to the deepest and best within us. When we can do this, inferiority complexes vanish because our inferiorities are no longer painful. None of us were meant to be all things. We were only meant to be ourselves—our best selves.

Light Up

I am going to write a list of words or phrases. They all have something in common. I think before too many are given you will be able to make the connection. Let's begin: playing the piano, dependability, acting skill, cheerfulness, writing well, friendliness, playing baseball, persistence (Have you figured it out yet?), an excellent memory, being a peacemaker.

By now the commonality should be evident. Each one of these words or phrases is a gift or talent. Some of them are not as obvious as others, and some are not even considered talents by many people. Those considered talents by everyone are obvious: playing the piano, skill in acting, writing well, athletic ability, an excellent memory. However, the other talents, even though not so obvious, are talents just the same: dependability, cheerfulness, friendliness, persistence, being a peacemaker.

I have heard a phrase repeated over and over again by young and old alike. It is generally expressed with either a wistful or somewhat bitter tone: "I don't have any talent!" Have any of us ever said that? "I don't have any talent." It is untrue, absolutely untrue.

I am reminded of the story of the young son of King Louis XVII of France. As a boy he had been taken by those who had dethroned his father. They thought that if they could destroy him morally, he would never be able to take his father's throne. So they set about to expose him to every filthy and vile temptation possible. But not once did the young prince yield. He held fast to his principles. After six months of such treatment he was asked why he would not submit to the filth all around him. His statement was classic. The boy said, "I cannot do what you ask, for I was born to be a king."

May I suggest that we too are of a royal lineage. We have heavenly parents. We are all children of God. Without being blasphemous, may I also suggest that our Heavenly Father, perfect and eternal, does not have untalented duds as offspring. Oh, he may have disobedient sons and daughters. He may have stubborn ones. But certainly from perfect parents must come children with talent and potential.

The Savior tried to teach that principle long ago. You will remember his parable:

"For the kingdom of heaven is as a man travelling into a far country, who called his own servants, and delivered unto them his goods.

"And unto one he gave five talents, to another two, and to another one; to every man according to his several ability; and straightway took his journey.

"Then he that had received the five talents went and traded with the same, and made them other five talents.

"And likewise he that had received two, he also gained other two.

"But he that had received one went and digged in the earth, and hid his lord's money.

"After a long time the lord of those servants cometh, and reckoneth with them." (Matthew 25: 14-19.)

You will also remember the end of the parable. The Lord praised both the servants who had been given five and two talents, and had doubled them, and he rewarded them accordingly. To the man who had hid his one talent, the Lord was severely displeased and gave him his just punishment.

Now, I find it significant that the parable of the talents does not consider the possibility of a servant with *no* talent. There is no such person. Everyone has talent. I repeat, every one of us has talent. Otherwise, the Lord would have given a parable of the "servant with no talent." Children of God all have talents.

After some reflection on this subject of talents and gifts, I have made several conclusions. The first one concerns awareness. I feel strongly that many of us only look for obvious talents which are already fully developed. Seldom is this the state talents are found in. Wolfgang Mozart, who composed a symphony at age eight, had an obvious talent. Helen Keller, deaf and blind, did not display much talent at that age because of her physical handicaps. Most of us fit somewhere between Mozart and Keller. We all have talents, but sometimes they must be discovered and then developed.

Let me illustrate my point with an example. It's about a boy called Tonio. As a young boy in Italy he was very unhappy because he could do nothing worthwhile except whittle wood. His two best friends were talented musicians. Everyone admired them. They often laughed at Tonio who could only whittle. They told him he was wasting his time and would never amount to anything. Tonio, himself, felt that he was not worth much.

One day he heard of a man who needed his talent of whittling. It was Amati, the greatest violin maker of his day. So Tonio went to work for him. He worked diligently and improved his skill in working with wood. He took great pride in whittling away just enough and yet not too much of the wood so the sound that came from the violins would be beautiful and rich. He learned to choose just the right type of wood and even chose with great care the glue to be used. He was never satisfied until a violin was as near perfect as he could make it. In time he became a far better maker of violins than his master, Amati. Today his instruments sell for hundreds of thousands of dollars. He is considered the greatest violin maker of all time. His last name was Stradivarius. Not bad for someone without obvious talent. To summarize my first point: we all have talents, obvious or not.

My second point concerns those of us with talents, but who encounter them in an unrefined state. I use another example. The great Polish pianist, Paderewski, always performed with amazing brilliance. After a particularly pleasing performance, an admirer came rushing up to him and said, "Oh, Mr. Paderewski, won't you please tell us the secret of your great genius?" "Certainly," replied the pianist with a gracious bow. "Eight hours a day of practice for twenty years."

Imagine what would happen if you and I practiced patience for eight hours a day for twenty years. Would our talent increase? What if we practiced virtue for twenty years? or dependability? or cheerfulness? or how about friendliness, kindness, or persistence? If we put our minds to it, we could develop any talent we cared to. Perhaps that talent would not be as evident as it is in others, but it would be there and it would be used. So to summarize my second point, since most of our talents are underdeveloped, we must begin now to practice them.

My third point is really a plea to get moving in the struggle to develop our gifts. Webster defines talent as "The abilities, powers, and gifts bestowed upon a man." Since those are divinely given, we should lose no time in our commitment to refine them. We have no idea how long our stewardship will last.

The older I grow, the more I am convinced that a talent or gift is much like a match. You know there are four characteristics about a simple match:

1. An unlit match is a yet-hidden power.

2. A match must be struck before its power can do any good.

3. The flame of a match can at first be destroyed with a small puff of air.

4. If the flame of a match is encouraged by placing it near more fuel with sufficient oxygen, it can grow into a mighty blaze.

It seems to me that a talent is like a match:

1. An undeveloped talent or gift is a yet-hidden power.

2. A talent must be tried before its power can do any good.

3. A talent, when first exposed or tried, can easily be destroyed by disuse or by criticism.

4. If the talent is improved by adding encouragement and practice, it can grow into a mighty power or force.

During my younger days I had the privilege of playing professional baseball. It was a blessing to me personally, but it also gave me a chance to watch men who had spent years developing their talents. It was a source of satisfaction to be around other young men who loved the game as I did, and who had worked hard. But I will also add that there were some who developed only their baseball talents. Patience, virtue and kindness were not always practiced. I felt sorry for those who were so one-sided. I believe the Lord intends that we develop several gifts, not just one. The more we practice many of them, the more we become like him.

Finally, the Lord wants us to be happy while we pursue our talents. And you will note the emphasis is on the plural form of that word. I have a friend at a local university who recently wrote of a person who did just that. Let me share with you his description.

"Whenever my car is sputtering and needs the careful diagnosis of a good mechanic, I take it to a particular friend of mine. This fellow's brothers all prepared for life by studying law, medicine, or engineering. But my friend just seemed to love to tinker with cars. He has his own automotive repair shop (rather small), and it is a joy to take a car to him for repairs. He is the picture of contentment because he is doing what he really enjoys doing. He bubbles with enthusiasm as he repairs an ailing part. He perpetually flashes a warm and genuine smile, and it is a complete joy to see how much he enjoys mending an automotive ailment. He's a very good mechanic, and each time I visit him I get the strong impression that he is much happier in life than his brothers who are in supposedly more lofty professions." (Joseph S. Wood, "Q and A," *The New Era*, March 1977, p. 12.)

I wish we could all catch the joy that comes when we happily pursue our life and our talents.

May I testify that the Lord has given each of us talents, that he expects us to develop them, and that by doing so we will enrich those around us as we prepare ourselves for that final accounting. May we realize we have talents and then set about to practice them consistently. We are *his* children. These are *his* gifts to us. May we understand that. May we "light up" our talents.

You're as Young as You Feel

I have often read in newspapers and magazines of prominent people who confess that they dread growing older. And it's a fear that's not confined to the famous. Wrinkle creams that guarantee unlined faces, hair coloring to dye those telltale gray locks, and cosmetic operations to lift faces sagged with years are quick sellers in our youth-conscious world. But, let's face it; dread it we may, but time is relentless and for all of us there will come a day when we wake up and discover we've joined the over-the-hill gang.

I think youth is grand, but I must admit I'm just the type to whistle, "I'm glad I'm not a teenager anymore." Birthdays are inevitable, and for those of us who may believe there's nothing to look forward to beyond thirty or forty or sixty-five, or whatever the magic age, life could run straight downhill. How foolish to mourn lost opportunities when every day is a new opportunity! How sad to look back on youth with its free flights of fancy and excitement as your happiest days when in reality happiness is intrinsically linked to maturity!

June Callwood wrote, "Lasting happiness depends on how much maturity a man has been able to assemble." In fact, she said, "Happy people can be any age, past twenty. Children are rarely happy: they have flights of joy, but their helplessness in a restrictive adult world keeps them close to despondency. Until their personalities stabilize, a process generally completed after the age of thirty-five, they are likely to be wretched with self-doubts and dismay at their inner muddle.

"Younger adults may describe themselves as 'happy'; it's a serviceable word to protect privacy. But many of them are frantic at the acceleration of time they are beginning to feel. They can sense the years wheeling by without any substantial or satisfying accomplishment....

"Yet all over the world, men and women, most of them in their thirties are turning a corner that they didn't see and stand transfixed by the miracle of finding themselves happy," said Callwood. "Nothing has changed in the room, in the family, nothing is different—but everything seems so. The personality has put together enough experience to make sane judgments, enough vitality to love, a few fragments of clarity and courage and a great deal of self-appraisal. There is a soundless click and a steady state of happiness ensues."

William Phelps, a noted educator, said the same kind of thing. "To say that youth is happier than maturity is like saying that the view from the bottom of the tower is better than the view from the top. As we ascend, the range of our view widens immensely, the horizon is pushed farther away. Finally as we reach the summit it is as if we had the world at our feet."

Think about it! Would you really trade the lessons

of your years, the wisdom of your seasons, the clarity and constancy and harmony of a well-defined identity for the intense, anxious pleasure of youth? Would any of us really go back to the days before words like compassion and justice—yes, and even sorrow—had a three-dimensional quality for us?

Age should only be hateful to us if it means the cessation of growth, the withering of dreams, the silence of feelings. And these qualities, after all, have nothing to do with chronology and everything to do with heart.

If you have the tendency the older you get to look at the young with longing eyes, if you find yourself dwelling on thoughts of illness and disease and exhaustion, if you find every experience a diminished thing, do not blame the years, blame yourself. Better yet, don't blame yourself, give yourself daily shots of enthusiasm.

Have you heard this excerpt from General MacArthur's credo: "Live with enthusiasm! Nobody grows old by merely living a number of years. People grow old only by deserting their ideals. Years wrinkle the skin but to give up enthusiasm wrinkles the soul.

"Worry, doubt, self-distrust, fear and despair— these bow the head and turn the growing spirit back to dust.

"Whether sixty or sixteen, there is in every being's heart the love of wonder, the sweet amazement at the stars and the starlike things and thoughts, the undaunted challenge of events, the unfailing child-like appetite for what-next, and the joy of the game of living.

"You are as young as your faith, as old as your doubt; as young as your self-confidence, as old as your fear; as young as your hope, as old as your despair.

"So long as your heart receives messages of

beauty, cheer, courage, grandeur and power from the earth, from man and from the infinite, so long are you young.

"When the wires are all down, and all the central places of your heart are covered with the snows of pessimism and the ice of cynicism, then, and only then, are you grown old indeed, and may God have mercy on your soul."

Live with enthusiasm, then, no matter what your age. A nineteenth-century Japanese artist wrote this at the age of seventy-five: "From the age of six I had a mania for drawing the forms of things. By the time I was fifty I had published an infinity of designs; but all I produced before seventy is not worth taking into account. At seventy-three I learned a little about the real structure of nature, of animals, plants, birds, fishes.

"In consequence, when I am eighty, I shall have made still more progress; at ninety I shall penetrate the mystery of things; at a hundred I shall certainly have reached a marvelous stage; and when I am a hundred and ten everything I do, be it but a dot, will be alive. I beg those who live as long as I do to see if I do not keep my word."

A man once observed, "Right now I'm eighteen years older than my father was when he died. And all of us kids thought he died of old age."

History abounds with people who as they got older, got better. Michelangelo, the famous sixteenth-century Italian artist, didn't undertake his monumental frescoed altar wall of the Sistine Chapel until he was sixty-nine years of age. When he died at ninety, he was still busy with his poetry, paintings and sculpture.

Goethe, the German genius of literature, didn't finish the classic *Faust* until he was eighty-one years old. He had begun it forty years earlier but when he came back to it, he had enhanced insight and freshness of imagination due to the extra years of living.

Herbert Hoover took on the job of coordinating world food supplies of thirty-eight countries for President Truman at the age of seventy-two. He was the United States Representative to Belgium at the age of eighty-four.

Thomas Edison was still inventing when past ninety; Benjamin Franklin was a key political figure and the wise, insightful diplomat for America when more than seventy-five years of age.

My own mother, now past eighty, still paints and gardens. Her paintings are sought-after masterpieces. Moses was over eighty when he led the Israelites.

Winston Churchill was sixty-five when he promised the British people his blood, toil, tears, and sweat in fighting World War II. Albert Schweitzer was in his eighties when roaming equatorial Africa, tending the sick, working on his manuscripts and playing Bach on his piano.

Colonel Sanders, who brought us his spicy Kentucky Fried Chicken, was living on a $105 a month social security check at the age of sixty-five when he discovered his famous recipe that brought him more than two million dollars.

Now, you might say, "But these people were extraordinary, gifted in ways beyond the average." But I say to you, the most extraordinary talent each of these had was enthusiasm, a flair for taking each new day with relish, a refusal to let wastelands of the soul develop and choke out all life while there's still life to be lived. You can do that too. You were meant to. As Ralph Waldo Emerson said, "We do not count a man's years, until he has nothing else to count."

God bless us so to do.

Slow Me Down, Lord

Have you ever had one of those days when you wanted to shout, "Stop the world, I want to get off!" It didn't stop though, did it? At least it never has for me. It just keeps moving right along. And in the process it takes us with it— seemingly faster every day.

In reflecting on the hectic pace we live, I found one of the finest bits of wisdom that I have encountered in some time. Reading these words by an unidentified author caused such a sense of relief that I pondered it, enjoyed it and resolved to change some things about my life because of it. I think we all could benefit from a daily review of its message:

"Slow me down, Lord!

"Ease the pounding of my heart by the quieting of my mind.

"Steady my hurried pace with vision of the eternal reach of time.

"Give me, amid the confusion of the day, the calmness of the everlasting hills.

"Break the tension of my nerves and muscles with the soothing music of the singing streams that live in my memory. Help me to know the magical, restoring power of sleep.

"Teach me the art of taking minute vacations—of slowing down to look at a flower, to chat with a friend, to pat a dog, to read a few lines from a good book.

"Slow me down, Lord, and inspire me to send my roots deep into the soil of life's enduring values that I may grow toward the stars of my greater destiny."

I submit that there has never been a generation of human beings that needed to hear those words quite like ours. Life is so short! It seems a shame to spend so much of it on the mundane. I am aware that we must work. I am aware that we must function in this incredibly chaotic world. But I am increasingly aware that some things really count, and some don't.

Homemakers will relate to the feeling of Donette Ockey who penned the following lines:

> One morning I woke and began resolutely
> To work till my tasks were done absolutely.
> I decided I would not waste even a minute—
> In the race against time, I determined to win it.
>
> I started all right, first clearing the dishes.
> Then saw it was time to clean the bowl for the
>   fishes.
> As I reached for the cleanser I thought that I'd
>   better
> Grab soap flakes as well for washing a sweater.
>
> As I went for the sweater, I saw that the bed
> Needed straightening, so stopped to do that
>   instead,
> But just then the phone rang, and while answering
>   it,
> I saw plants on the sill that needed watering a bit.

So went my day, and I worked till bone tired;
Then happy and proud, I sat back and admired.
But taking stock of my home, my joy soon
    diminished;
Everything was started, but nothing was finished.
(Donette V. Ockey, "Don't Interrupt Yourself.")

Men have experienced the same feeling of frustration, either at home or at work—or both. We've all gotten our projects started early in the morning and then felt utter frustration when nothing was really finished at the day's end. But may I remind you that if we take a little different approach, even our unfinished projects can be looked at in perspective. Remember those opening lines from "Slow Me Down, Lord"? If that housewife would take just a few moments to "slow down" perhaps her poem would read something like this:

Thank God for dirty dishes,
They have a tale to tell;
While other folks go hungry
We're eating very well.
With home and health and happiness
We shouldn't want to fuss,
For by this stack of evidence
God's very good to us.
(From Daryl Hoole, "Thank God for Dirty Dishes,"
The Art of Homemaking.)

So what if the housework isn't all done? So what if the office work isn't finished? And what if you don't make it to that meeting? And who cares if it's 10:00 P.M. and the homework isn't completed? (Besides your teachers, that is.) Let's be diligent! Let's do our best! Let's use time wisely! But, let's slow down!

In one of our penitentiaries is a sign made by the inmates. Its meaning is doubled because of its loca-

tion. It reads: "Don't serve time. Let time serve you."
We don't need to go to prison to understand the implications of that motto. Some of us are already
prisoners. The bars may be missing, but our confine-
ment is real. Time is our warden, and in some cases,
our executioner. Although I believe in sustaining the
law, we need to break out of our cell. Some of us need
to literally cry out, "slow me down, Lord."

Then we need to go to work in using our time more
wisely—or should I say more slowly. If we're too
hurried to hug a kid, hold hands with our spouse,
romp with the dog, play games on a Saturday, enjoy
some tennis, read a book, do some knitting, or just sit
and think—we're too busy.

Ralph Waldo Emerson and Solomon both gave us
great advice. First, Emerson: "Guard well your spare
moments."

And from Solomon: "To every thing there is a
season, and a time to every purpose under the
heaven" (Ecclesiastes 3:1).

If we put those two together, we come up with a
pretty good formula for using our time wisely. Since
everything has its appropriate time, including our
work, we need to guard our spare moments very carefully. In fact, we need to make sure we have some
spare moments every day.

Now, may I suggest that some of those spare
moments be used on us—for our welfare. I don't think
that's a selfish attitude, I think it's a must. How about
a few moments

In morning prayers,
In pondering,
In scripture reading,
In taking a walk,
In writing a letter.

We can add or subtract at will, but there are some spiritual realities about our spare moments that we need to weigh carefully.

And then, of course, we need to use some of our spare moments for others. Several of those possibilities we've already suggested.

We *can* slow down and we *can* learn to enjoy our life. It's up to us. May we understand that taking time to slow down will speed up our chances for happiness now and eternal life in the world to come.

A Round Tuitt

The other day I found on my desk a single sheet of paper with a two-word headline, "Important Notice!" That kind of announcement always catches my attention and so I read with interest the following declaration: "The management regrets that it has come to their attention that employees dying on the job are failing to fall down. This practice must stop, as it becomes impossible to distinguish between death and natural movement of the staff. Any employee found dead in an upright position will be dropped from the payroll."

I chuckled when I read the notice. Some people procrastinate *everything,* even falling down when they ought to. I can well imagine some companies having to fold if that proclamation were adhered to.

It is that very thing that I want to call attention to—procrastination—or better still, the lack of it.

In the scriptures we are given this wise advice

about taking advantage of our greatest gift—time: "This is the day which the Lord hath made; we will rejoice and be glad in it" (Psalm 118:24).

You and I have each day in which we can do what we want. We can accomplish, serve, grow; or we can sit, dream, squander. Now, I'll be the first to admit that the latter alternative isn't all that unattractive, but when there are things to do that really need to be done, choosing that alternative can be a disaster.

Just a minute ago we read some excellent counsel from the scriptures. Let's consider now the opposite viewpoint:

> The devil decided to come out one day
> And consult with two imps while they were at play.
> "I want you two helpers to give me a plan
> That will bring down to hell each woman and
>   man."

> The first imp thought, and then he said,
> "My plan will get man to hell when he's dead.
> Let's tell mankind that there could not be
> A heaven, nor hell, nor eternity.

> "And what a man wants he can go out and steal;
> He can covet and lie, be immoral, and kill."
> But the devil said quickly, "Man isn't that dumb.
> We'd get quite a few, but not every last one.

> "I want a good plan that will capture them all
> And entice all mankind to sin and to fall."
> The second imp said, "I know a way—
> Just get mankind to put off each day

> "His repentance to the God up above,
> Their creator and Savior who is full of love.
> Let us go out, and the world we will tell
> 'There is a heaven, there is a hell.'

"Let's tell them the truth—they must not commit
    sin,
For if they don't repent, their souls Satan will win.
But don't worry today to repent and do good;
Just wait till tomorrow to do as you should.

"When another day comes, you'll have plenty of
    time
To do the Lord's work and to 'let your light shine.'
Put off good today and do it tomorrow
For time is one thing you always can borrow."

The devil then said, with a wink of his eye,
"Now that is a plan I think I can buy.
Tell man to procrastinate repenting today,
And eat, drink, and be merry, and go on his way.

"And soon man will see it's too late to repent
And he has been fooled by the evil serpent."
We now know the story of the devil so sly.
So repent now, not later—live with God when you
    die.
(Ron J. Whitehead, "Procrastination.")

May I suggest that learning to use our time wisely
will not only thwart the adversary, but will bring us a
great feeling of self-worth. And, in addition, those
around us will be blessed. I'm not an advocate of
spending every waking moment "doing something."
There are surely times to rest, to think, to ponder, to
recreate; but Satan understands that if he can get us to
put off the things that are really important he may well
have stopped our progress—perhaps for good.

So, the questions we ask ourselves are, "What do
we do about it? How do we change, if we need to?"

About a year ago, I received a copy of one of the
most clever ideas I have ever seen. It was simply a
piece of paper cut into a circle. On one side of the circle

of paper was its title: "A Round Tuitt." I was informed that with my round piece of paper, I was finally getting "Around-To-It."

I submit that we all need "A Round Tuitt." And if we do, the instructions I found on the other side of my "Tuitt" answer our question, "How do I change?" Let me share the advice:

"Have you ever said, 'I'll do it when I get around to it'? Well, here it is—A ROUND TUITT. It will help you achieve in this life, accomplish your goals, provide that element which nothing else has been able to provide. It's the key to open all locks.

"Think of the adventure. With 'A Round Tuitt,' you can become a well rounded individual capable of unlimited heights of accomplishment. You carry your destiny within your own hands.

"You no longer have to be shy of time. You now have 'A Round Tuitt' to help you get more out of those daily twenty-four hours.

"Directions for the use of 'A Round Tuitt' are simple: Grasp it and go! Don't worry about those who say, 'It can't be done,' 'I don't have the time,' . . . 'Wait until tomorrow.'

"With 'A Round Tuitt' your motto becomes: 'Do It Now!'

"Remember, the key to reaching your goal is: You must first get 'A Round Tuitt.'

"P.S. What are you waiting for?"

Isn't that great? This is the key! We need to stop procrastinating. We must decide that now is the time to get around to it and then learn to *do it*. First, however, I suggest that we each take the counsel given in Psalms: "I thought on my ways" (Psalm 119:59). Let's take some time to think about what we're doing. Do we need to improve? In what areas? What is the price? Are we really serious about it? Having done so and having made a commitment, we can apply the second part of the scripture: "I made haste, and delayed not to keep thy commandments" (Psalm 119:60).

In other words, if we're really going to stop our procrastinating and do better, let's start with areas that are truly important. I submit that to do otherwise is like going into battle with a golf club (although some say that when I golf, it *is* a battle). A golf club may be all right in certain instances, but for saving your life, you may want to choose something more appropriate.

And what are the appropriate and important things in our lives on which we would want to focus our energies? May I suggest just a few?

- Living the commandments, especially the basic ten. If we don't do that, little else matters.
- Spending more time with our wives or husbands.
- Taking time with each of our children each day.
- Improving our education.
- Making our homes more attractive.
- Starting an exercise program.

The list is as long or as short as we make it. The important thing is that we begin.

Since by-and-by never comes, may we decide that now is indeed the time to start or stop doing things we know need to be changed. I know we can! I am positive we should. I am determined we will. May the Lord bless us with the courage to make changes where they're needed, and to make them now. I love the Lord for his patience, and pray that where necessary, we may indeed get "A Round Tuitt."

Taking Advantage

I must confess that I am slightly prejudiced toward the fairer sex. Not only did I marry one of the choicest of all God's creations, but I also had the privilege of helping to rear three wonderful daughters. All are now married and doing well. There were times however...

I admit that my bias showed through as I gathered material for this book. I felt impressed to look for some ideas concerning time—how to take advantage of it. You've heard the ominous warning many times: "before it's too late!" My reflection on how quickly my daughters went from eight to eighteen intensified my search. May I interpret, parenthetically, that some of those teenage years seemed rather long. As I remember them, each of my daughters' sixteenth year lasted about twenty-seven months, or so it seemed. But, generally, the years flew by.

As I pondered and searched I found some things I would like to share along with a few of my observations. I want you to remember that the theme of "Taking Advantage" is especially dedicated to those who have had, or do have, or will have daughters.

This swift passage of time is a common experience. One minute it's "good morning" and the next moment it's "goodnight." Life is here one moment and the next thing you know, it's gone. Sometimes it lasts a full ninety years. Sometimes it lasts only a second.

If we were smarter, we would take advantage of the time. I suggest we all get smarter.

Job of old asked a profound question: "Is there not an appointed time to man upon earth?" (Job 7:1.) Then, of course, the question is answered affirmatively. Man's time *is* measured. And since it is, the Lord gave a wise commandment. He said: "Thou shalt not idle away thy time" (D&C 60:13).

I suppose the Lord could have worded that commandment any way he wished. But what that says to me is that we ought to be taking advantage of our time.

Now, what should we be doing? Is reading a good book a waste of time? Or is a game of tennis a no-no? Is it work and no play? The Lord's answer rings out with a resounding *no*!

"To every thing there is a season, and a time to every purpose under the heaven:

"A time to be born, and a time to die; a time to plant, and a time to pluck up that which is planted;

"A time to kill, and a time to heal; a time to break down, and a time to build up;

"A time to weep, and a time to laugh; a time to mourn, and a time to dance;

"A time to cast away stones, and a time to gather stones together; a time to embrace, and a time to refrain from embracing;

"A time to get, and a time to lose; a time to keep, and a time to cast away;

"A time to rend, and a time to sew; a time to keep silence, and a time to speak;

"A time to love, and a time to hate; a time of war, and a time of peace." (Ecclesiastes 3:1-8.)

Without being presumptuous, let me rephrase that great scripture from Ecclesiastes in current language.

To everything there is a season, and a time to every purpose under the heaven:

A time to go to work and a time to stay at home with the family.

A time to go to the movies and a time to read stories to the kids.

A time to go out with the family to a restaurant and a time to stay home and help with the dishes.

A time to reprimand the kids and a time to frankly admit "I was wrong."

A time to be together as a family and a time to get the wife out of the house.

A time to show great emotional strength and a time to let your kids see you cry.

A time to laugh until you think you'll die and a time to hug your kids until they think they will.

A time to realize that eternity will last forever and a time to recognize that today is the most important of them all.

I repeat, if we were smarter we would take advantage of our time. That is, we would take advantage of our time to do things that are really important—things like a piggyback ride, an eternal game of Monopoly, a family ride in the car (at least three blocks and back), a picnic in the backyard, a date with your spouse, a race to the mailbox, a family prayer, a good-night kiss. Things that count.

Let me use one of those "all-girl" quotes I was telling you about. It is a final, gentle reminder of how fast time goes. Harry Jones describes the swift-moving change of a girl to adolescence.

"Adolescence is almost as quick as darkness after daylight. One day a daughter is reading *Nancy Drew;* the next day she is reading all those magazines with Donny Osmond on the cover.

"Yesterday she walked to the store to browse the candy counter for a Hershey bar or a Tootsie Roll. Today she is browsing the perfume counter for such things as 'Summer Night,' or some such interesting, exotic name.

"Yesterday she went to the doctor—or had to be dragged is a better description. She said she might faint if she had a flu shot along with the rest of the family. She was the only one who cried. Today she wants to have her ears pierced!

"Yesterday she warmed up for dinner by eating an ice-cream cone and a candy bar just before the table was set. She still ate everything on her plate and leftovers others would give her. Today she won't eat bread, potatoes, pie or any desserts. She will pick at her food like a sick canary. Every two minutes she will ask if the rest of the family thinks she is too fat.

"Yesterday it was a fifteen-minute argument to get her to run a comb through her hair. Now she combs it twenty-one times a day, worries about split ends and asks how the rest of the family thinks she would look as a redhead.

"Yesterday she played football and kick-the-can. Today she worries about her knees being bony and her feet being too large.

"Yesterday she could see a country mile. She had eyes like a hawk. Suddenly she needs contact lenses and a pair of dark glasses with the lens as big around as a cup. Her eyes must be shielded from the sun even on rainy days."

And may I add, yesterday she took my love for granted and my time simply because she was small.

Today she must be *shown* that I love her and have more time spent with her because there's so little left before she's grown.

Remember that taking advantage of our time now will ensure an eternity of happiness. May we be wise enough to enjoy our greatest possessions—our families. Now! No matter how old they are. God intends it so.

II
Those Close

Seeing a Sermon

On one of my trips, I encountered a fine little chap about four years old and proceeded to ask him questions:

"How old are you?"

"Four."

"What's your name?"

"Steven."

"Do you go to school?"

"Nope!"

"Do you want to?"

"Yup!"

"Do you have brothers and sisters?"

"Yup!"

"Do you like them?"

(Silence)

After that stimulating conversation, I pursued the question I really wanted to ask: "What do you want to be when you grow up?" His answer: "Just like my dad!"

Now, that may not have been the answer I expected, but it undoubtedly pleased his father, who beamed at his son's good taste. I had to smile just to look at the two of them. What is the old saying? "Out of the mouths of babes..."

That little boy said more than he realized, and although that father was pleased, I am not sure he fully understood the responsibility his son placed squarely on his broad shoulders. In fact, it is probably good he doesn't. If any of us were truly aware of the implications of our actions on others, we probably wouldn't sleep very well at night. In some respects, ignorance is bliss.

Unfortunately, in some cases, ignorance is definitely *not* bliss. Let me share with you a letter from another little fellow, Tommy. I don't know where the letter comes from, or even if it is technically true, but in reality, the spirit of the letter has been written by more kids than we will probably ever know. Here is the letter:

"Dear Jesus:

"My name is Tommy. I am six. I go to school. So does Suzy. She's my friend, we get along good. She lives in the yellow house on the corner. My house is green. I'm going to marry her when I grow up. We go to Sunday School together and lots of other places too.

"I really don't like Sunday 'cause I have to put on icky clothes. Suzy too. But we both like one part, when they tell us stories about Jesus. That's you! And this is what I've learned about you.

"Jesus was my brother. He died and flew to heaven on a big white cloud. I'd like to do that. It would be better than flying on a plane. Suzy says she'd be afraid. I wouldn't. I'm not afraid of anything.

"Jesus also said to love everybody and do what mommy and daddy says and if the little kid who's only three years old wants to play with your toys, we should share. He also says that fighting is no good and we shouldn't tell things that aren't true. He says not to do anything noisy on Sunday, 'cause that's the day that is his—just like Saturday is my day to play. He said not to call names.

"But Suzy and I don't understand. Mommy and daddy said that we should do all these things, but yesterday I heard mommy call Mrs. Thomas a mean old woman, and a nagging old hag. And daddy said that he couldn't understand how anybody could love Mr. Smith 'cause he sure couldn't. And Suzy said she heard her mommy scream at her daddy and when we collected pennies for the crippled children, some grown-up people said that the children had to take care of themselves, 'cause they had no money to share. And Suzy said that her mommy told her there were no more cookies when Suzy knew there were. And daddy watches loud football games on TV on Sunday and yells.

"So Suzy and I talked it over and we decided that you're just for little kids and when we get big we can't do it anymore. Jesus, you must have a new set of rules for them—anyway, yesterday, mommy told me I was a big boy. So, sorry Jesus, I love you but I've outgrown you.

"Love,
"Tommy"

A great prophet, Jacob, placed the responsibility (and sometimes blame) right where it belongs: "Ye have broken the hearts of your tender wives, and lost the confidence of your children, because of your bad example before them" (Jacob 2:35).

That is just one side of the coin—a bad example. The other side of the coin can be as dramatic and up-lifting as the other can be harmful. Let me cite an

example—a good example. You golfers can identify
with this one.

It has been my pleasure to share the fairways and
greens (and in my case a few lonely sand traps) with
some of the world's best: Larry Nelson and Lee
Trevino. But one of the finest examples I have seen
was set by Billy Casper, a gentleman as well as a
golfer. While playing the Bing Crosby Tournament at
Pebble Beach, he was disqualified during the final
round. That is a rare occurrence for the top pros. But
the reason was as rare as the disqualification—his
caddie failed to make the tee-off time.

Billy's caddy had a legitimate reason for his ten-
minute delay, but it cost his boss a few thousand
dollars. Now, how would you have felt if it had been
your caddie? Some golfers would have buried their
caddies in the deepest sand trap. But not Billy Casper.
When asked by the press if he was angry, he said
simply, "You see, in a situation like that, I was worried
about his welfare more than anything else." Then he
made it a point to sit down privately with his caddie
and talk to him about the mistake. Later on, when
asked once more about the incident, Billy assured both
the interviewer and his caddie with this comment:
"Not only will he be caddie for me in this one [tourna-
ment] but I hope for the next 10 or 12 years" (Milton
Richman, UPI sports writer). Now that is what I call a
great public example!

I really believe that the Lord's injunction about
example is as appropriate today as it was then: "Let
your light so shine before men that they may see your
good works, and glorify your Father which is in
heaven" (Matthew 5:16).

You see, every time we set a good example for our
family, or friends, or whoever, we bring honor to ourselves, our families and to our heavenly parents. Every

positive example brings joy to our maker. After all, they are his children we set the examples for.

May I suggest that we each take a good look at the example we are setting. Can we improve? Can parents be more careful about what they say and do around those impressionable kids? And teenagers, don't kid yourselves, your example *does* affect your parents. I know! A friend of mine recently complained that his children's constant rock music was beginning to take its toll—he was beginning to like it. He wanted some kind of vaccination to stop it before it went too far.

I have known some teenagers who have literally become the salvation of their parents because of their example. It works in every association: parents to kids; kids to parents; brother to sister and vice versa; neighbors to neighbors; friends to friends; strangers to strangers. It is a wonderful cycle.

May I conclude with a poem by Edgar A. Guest. It is a great one!

> I'd rather see a sermon than to hear one any day,
> I'd rather one should walk with me than merely tell the way;
> The eye's a better pupil and more willing than the ear,
> Fine counsel is confusing, but example's always clear;
> And the best of all the preachers are the men who live their creeds,
> For to see God put in action is what everybody needs.
> I can soon learn how to do it, if you'll let me see it done,
> I can watch your hands in action, but your tongue too fast may run;
> And the lectures you deliver may be very wise and true,

But I'd rather get my lesson by observing what you
    do;
For I may misunderstand you and the high advice
    you give,
But there's no misunderstanding how you act and
    how you live.
(Edgar A. Guest, "The Living Sermon.")

Now, may the Lord bless us to look carefully at our example. And may he also give us strength to follow only those that will bring credit to us all, especially our Heavenly Father. I bear you my witness that we are watched by some whose lives we will profoundly affect. And some are those of whom we are not even aware. And, finally, I leave you my assurance that we are also watched by him. May we please him as we set great examples for his children.

Seventy Times Seven

Those of you who like to take tests and quizzes will enjoy the one I am about to administer. If you never enjoyed that part of learning, you should still feel quite comfortable because you can't fail. Those are the kind of tests I enjoy. There are only seven questions, but they are important. If you can respond no to each of the seven, please hold onto a piece of furniture, otherwise you may be taken to heaven. Here are the seven questions:

1. Do you ever say, "Well, I will forgive you but I can never forget"?

2. Are you ever secretly happy when something unfortunate happens to someone you do not like?

3. Is there anyone you avoid or refuse to speak to?

4. When you get angry with someone, do you sulk —even for days?

5. Do you secretly take satisfaction when you think they may be headed straight to...that lower kingdom?

6. Do you ever talk sarcastically to others about someone you think has offended you?

7. When you argue with a family member, do you bring up the past in order to make them angry?

How did you do? I know how well I did. In which direction did you feel yourself being pulled? Luckily, there will be a make-up test given often during our lives. But I'm a firm believer in passing tests as quickly as possible. I never did like to take a late make-up exam and then wonder if I was going to pass or not. So, why not start preparing for a passing grade right now.

John Greenleaf Whittier tells of someone, perhaps himself, who made that decision in an instant. It's a great poem and many will recognize it:

> My heart was heavy, for its trust had been
> Abused, its kindness answered with foul wrong;
> So turning gloomily from my fellow men,
> One summer sabbath day I strolled among
> The green mounds of the village burial place;
> Where, pondering how all human love and hate
> Find one sad level; and how, soon or late,
> Wronged and wrongdoer, each with meekened
>   face,
> And cold hands folded over a still heart,
> Pass the threshold of our common grave,
> Whither all footsteps tend, whence none depart,
> Awed for myself, and pitying my race,
> Our common sorrow, like a mighty wave,
> Swept all my pride away, and trembling, I forgave.

May I suggest that one of the greatest tests of our lives will be that described by Whittier. Can we learn to forgive—really forgive? some men? all men? That's tough, but if we want a passing grade, we'll just have to learn to do it.

Let me ask another question. Have you ever forgiven someone (a spouse, a child, a parent, a brother or sister, a friend, or even an enemy) and then had them turn around and do the same thing all over again? Exasperating, isn't it? Well, what did you do then? Not long ago I heard an upset father say to his daughter, "Well, that's it! I've overlooked that same thing a hundred times. No more! Don't try that 'sorry' bit on me again. It won't work!"

Peter once asked the Savior about that kind of problem, and he received a well-known response.

"Then came Peter to him, and said, Lord, how oft shall my brother sin against me, and I forgive him? till seven times?

"Jesus saith unto him, I say not unto thee, Until seven times: but, Until seventy times seven." (Matthew 18:21-22.)

That's pretty sobering—seventy times seven. When you figure that out it comes to 490. At one forgiveness per day (for the same weakness), I figured it would take approximately one year and four months and then the obligation to forgive is over. Then, let them have it!

We both know that the Lord didn't mean that at all. He meant that we should forgive as often as necessary. That may be many more times than seventy times seven. And it may be difficult—very difficult—to do. Let me illustrate:

"On the afternoon of Sept. 6, 1901, United States President William McKinley held a public reception at the Pan-American exposition in Buffalo, New York. Hundreds of people came to shake hands with him and wish him well.

"One young man, however, brought no good wishes for the president. He waited in line with a pistol hidden in a bandage around his right hand. As he approached the head of the reception line, he fired a bullet which hit the president.

"As William McKinley fell to the floor mortally

wounded, he pointed to Leon Czolgosz, the assassin, who had already been seized by onlookers. 'Don't let them hurt him,' whispered the injured president.'' (Arthur S. Anderson, "They Taught Forgiveness," *The Instructor,* June 1959, p. 190.)

I call that returning good for evil, and it is, I really believe, a mark of greatness.

Now, let's get even more practical for a moment. I'm going to share a passage from Matthew, chapter 5. As you read it you'll be tempted to say "What has that got to do with being 'practical'?" I'll explain. First, the scripture:

"Therefore if thou bring thy gift to the altar, and there rememberest that thy brother hath ought against thee;

"Leave there thy gift before the altar, and go thy way; first be reconciled to thy brother, and then come and offer thy gift." (Matthew 5:23-24.)

Did you get that? When *we* have been offended, *we* should take the initiative and go to our brother and be reconciled, and not vice versa. I submit that if we begin to do that now, it will be about the most practical thing we can do to start learning about forgiveness. Imagine, when we are offended, *we* go and seek *him!* Try it! President Lincoln did.

"Even in war, Lincoln was more lenient toward his enemies than most politicians are in peace.

"Indeed, even at the height of the hostilities, Lincoln once uttered a few kind words about the confederates and a woman in the audience stood up and demanded to know how he could speak kindly of his enemies when he should rather destroy them.

"Lincoln paused, and then drawled, 'What madam, do I not destroy them when I make them my friends?'" (Sydney Harris, *Deseret News.*)

I again suggest that if you and I will start returning good for evil by making the first move toward those who offend us, we won't have many enemies, if any at all.

In conclusion, let me suggest three practical reminders of what we can do to get ready for our make-up exam:

1. Let's try our best not to offend — especially our own family members.

2. When someone apologizes and asks for forgiveness, let's do it cheerfully.

3. Let's start making the first move to become reconciled to those who offend us.

These principles really do work — when they're applied.

Someday, you and I are going to stand before our Lord to be judged. I bear testimony that he's a loving God, but I also witness that he is just. If we are forgiven by him as we forgive others, how will we do? Let's make sure we're on good terms with him.

Paul Boese said, "Forgiveness does not change the past, but it does enlarge the future." In fact, it enlarges eternity for those who learn to do it now.

May we actually, daily, do it. I know we can. Let's reach out for those who have offended us, even as the Lord reaches out for us. We'll find greater happiness than we ever expected.

In Good Company

I would like to quote something that will give away your age. If you can remember this little item you are definitely over forty. If you don't recognize it—well, I think you will find it interesting. It is from a radio and television series called "My Friend Irma." Now, I could sing it for you, but if my memory serves me correctly the FCC has certain standards which must be met. Here is the little theme song which was used at the beginning and end of every production:

> Friendship, friendship,
> Just a perfect friendship.
> When other friendships have been forgot,
> Ours will still be hot!

That may be grammatically incorrect, but it is definitely true. Somehow there are friendships that fade with time. Then there are others which will last eternally. I think we have all experienced both kinds, but it is the second type for which I will be everlastingly grateful. Those friendships come in all shapes and sizes, in all colors and for various reasons.

A friend of mine once asked a number of people of different ages who they considered to be their best friend, and why. The answers, starting with an eight-year-old girl, went something like this.

"'Who is your best friend?' 'My mommie,' she replied. 'Why?' 'Because she is nice to me.'

"A [teenage] . . . young man was asked the same question. 'My bishop.' 'Why?' 'Because he listens to us guys.'

"A 19-year-old girl: 'My teacher.' 'Why?' 'She is always available to me, even after class.'

"A 13-year-old boy: 'My Scoutmaster.' 'Why?' 'He does everything with us.'

"A prisoner: 'The chaplain.' 'Why?' 'He believes me. He even believed me sometimes when he shouldn't have.'

"A husband: 'My wife.' 'Why?' 'Because she is the best part of me.'" (Marvin J. Ashton, "What Is a Friend?" *Ensign*, January 1973, p. 43.)

Those are great answers!

I submit that we all need friends. Rather, I should say we all need *good* friends. We need friends who lift us up and make us better.

I suppose there are some who really believe they can make it on their own; that they don't need to rely on anyone but themselves. And I guess there are some who can actually do it that way. But what a waste! They choose to eliminate the very thing that brings joy to life. They eat their potatoes all right, but they refuse gravy or butter or salt or pepper, or anything that would season their lives and make them enjoyable.

The spirit of what I am saying is found in the old story of the horse. I have shared it before. You will recall it is about the farmer who had a horse which he always entered in the horse races during fair week. The horse was not a runner; it could hardly keep up with itself. But every year the farmer's horse was in the race. So one time his neighbor said to him, "Bill, why are you always entering that horse of yours in the race? You know it cannot win a race." He said, "I know, but I like to see him get all lathered up in good company."

Well, that is how I feel about friendship. It's great just to be in good company. It makes you feel better about yourself, and about humanity. I know that sometimes friendships will not be reciprocated, but for every friend who disappoints you there will be others who will not.

Ralph Waldo Emerson gave probably the best known key to friendship. It bears repeating: "The only way to have a friend is to be one." That sounds like a pretty good place to start—with me, with you...with us reaching out.

The story of David and Jonathan is a classic. If you'll recall, Jonathan was technically the heir to Saul's throne. But David was chosen by the Lord and anointed by the Prophet Samuel to replace the aging king. And yet, Jonathan risked his life to save his friend, David. He helped him, he protected him, he comforted him, he defended him. And most of all, he loved him. The scriptures describe their relationship in these words:

"And it came to pass...that the soul of Jonathan was knit with the soul of David, and Jonathan loved him as his own soul" (1 Samuel 18:1).

And, most important of all, theirs was a friendship of *mutual* love and respect.

Now, finally, let me mention a quality of friendship that we don't talk about very often. We ought to, but we don't. I sometimes think we are afraid to. But most happily married couples understand this principle. The Lord understands it too because it is included in the wisdom of Proverbs. Let me quote it: "Faithful are the wounds of a friend" (Proverbs 27:6).

"You mean to say that a real friend will wound another friend?" That's right! But the wound will be faithful. It will be to help, not hurt. It will be to correct, not criticize. It will be kind, not cruel. As Aristotle put it: "Friends are an aid to the young, to guard them from error...." If we see that a friend is about to be hit by a truck, we don't silently say, "I sure hope he sees it. I'd tell him myself but I don't want to hurt him by telling him. I wouldn't offend him for the world!" What we do is yell "Look out!" And if we yell quickly enough, it may do some good.

May I suggest that to warn a friend, or to suggest that he may be making a mistake, takes courage. But friendships built on that kind of concern are the only kind to have. Even yelling "Look out!" doesn't have to be shouted in anger. But it surely must be shouted.

I remember the story of the Morrison-Knudsen team. When Morrison was barely out of his teens, he approached Knudsen and asked to go into business with him. Knudsen owned a few horses and was building a road to a dam. Although surprised, he asked Morrison what he had to offer. Morrison responded, "Plenty of grit." "I mean how much money?" "No money, just grit!" Well, it was a lasting partnership. That's what it takes to make an eternal friendship — grit. We need the courage to say what we need to say to protect those who call us friends.

I love my wife. She and I are friends. She corrects me as often as needed, which is more often than I would like to admit. But she loves me enough to do it.

I bear witness that our Father loves us. And when necessary, he does the same with us. We would do well to follow his example. May we do so! May we be faithful friends. May we understand that those kinds of friendships will bring happiness now and eternal associations in the world to come.

Bumper Stickers

Have you hugged your broker today?" That was on a bumper sticker I saw one day. I smiled when I saw it because I realized that it was a takeoff on the original, "Have you hugged your kids today?"

I'm a confessed bumper sticker watcher. They say as much about the owner of the car as they do in giving information. I read them all—well, almost all. There are some that are better not read. After a while you get so you can tell if they're going to be readable or not.

Bumper stickers range from the funny to the religious, from political to commercial. Teenagers use them; young adults use them; middle-aged people use them; even the older generation use them. You can tell who's in the car when you see this sticker: "Happiness is being a grandparent." And then there's the oldie but goodie you find on a dilapidated VW Bug which proclaims, "My other car is a Porsche."

Bumper stickers are interesting to read and

generally are positive, if not uplifting. Not too long ago I read a short statement on bumper stickers by a noted psychiatrist. He said:

"Bumper stickers are a form of personal expression, but a curious one. Unlike graffiti, which are completely anonymous, bumper stickers say, 'This is me, but I don't have to look you in the eye to say it.' The bumper sticker is a kind of passive declaration for folks who want to identify with something but don't want to get involved personally." (Dr. William Flynn, as quoted in *Reader's Digest*, August 1979.) Not a bad observation!

When I read that commentary by Dr. Flynn, I began to see the application in another area that has been on my mind lately. One phrase in particular stood out as I read it: "The bumper sticker is a kind of passive declaration for folks who...don't want to get involved."

Then this thought occurred to me: What if we reversed that phrase? What if bumper stickers were used as an *active* declaration by folks who want to be *personally* involved? And what if we made those stickers verbal as well as written? I guess what I am suggesting is the use of small phrases, whether written or verbal, to compliment and lift those around us. We could make a habit of handing out bumper stickers every day—a short compliment here, a precise pat on the back there. It would do wonders for family members. Those bumper stickers might sound something like this: "Gee, you look nice." Or, how about this one: "That tasted great." Then add any number you want: "The house sure looks nice." "I'm really proud of you." "Those are great grades." "You did your best." The list is as long as your imagination. Those bumper stickers could be handed out to anyone, anytime. Pick the time; pick the place. As the Lord said in

Proverbs: "A word spoken in due season, how good is it!" (Proverbs 15:23.)

There is a challenge, however. In order to give them out, we're going to have to start paying attention to the good going on around us. I suppose that there are some reading this who know someone who has very few redeeming qualities. But if you look hard enough you can always find good.

I am reminded of one shy teenage boy who was told that to be polite, he should always give his date a compliment—a "bumper sticker" if you will. This young man attended a school dance and managed to say something positive about each girl he danced with. However, with one particularly robust girl he found nothing positive to compliment. Finally, at the end of the dance and in desperation, he blurted, "Gee, for a heavy girl, you don't sweat much!" You see what I mean? We can find something positive to say about everyone.

Now, those daily bumper stickers can be written as well as spoken. One creative young man at a nearby university used the card section during the halftime at a football game to proclaim something he was afraid to say in person. Sitting in the stands on the opposite side of the card section, his girl was shocked to read the message, "Julie, I love you." Then the cards flipped over and she read the question, "Will you marry me?" Guess what she did?

On a more serious note, such written bumper stickers can literally save lives. A good father watched as his son struggled with some temptations that were becoming too big to handle. Unable to verbally say what he wanted, he pinned the following note on his son's pillow:

"Dear Son:

"This will only be a short note, but I have wanted

to tell you something personally for a long time, but for some reason I find that hard to do.

"I know I haven't been the best father in the world, but it isn't because I don't care about you. My biggest frustration is that I do care very much, and yet I just can't get the words out.

"I know you have been struggling lately with some personal challenges, and I have been silently watching from the sidelines. This may not be getting in the game, exactly, but I just had to let you know how I feel.

"Son, I love you. I'm proud of you. And I know you'll make the right decisions. A father couldn't have a better son. I'll try to do better in supporting you. Please let me help if I can.

> "Love,
> "Dad"

This young man and his father met in the hall a few minutes later. It would be impossible to describe the sacredness of the encounter. A boy was saved by a dad who wrote what he could not say. Job hit it squarely on the head: "How forcible are right words!" (Job 6:25.) If we can't say it, why not post it. The results are often the same.

May I encourage us all to take time daily to spread "bumper stickers." I know that if we will do so, our wives and husbands, and our children in particular, will be made immeasurably more happy. And that's what life is all about.

May I share my witness that seeing the good in others is only half the assignment. Let's also tell them. Such procedures won't leave time to do much worrying about others' faults—only our own.

May we be wise enough to do so. And by so doing may we receive our own bumper sticker from the Lord. And may it read, "Well done, thou good and faithful servant" (Matthew 25:21).

Tattle Tales

While living in Massachusetts for a couple of years, I had the opportunity of reviewing some of the great incidents and landmarks of our country's early history. What a privilege that was! But of all those sites and stories, one of the most sobering to me concerned the witch hunts in Salem. And, in particular, one true story sticks in my mind to this day. It involved a group of young girls who decided they were going to destroy several of the "sisters" of that community. It was not difficult to do in the hysteria of those late 1600s. A few well-placed rumors and several women were hanged. Of those innocently executed, one was the great-great-great-grandmother of a good friend of mine. That coincidence makes the story easy for me to remember.

Now, a very good question is, Why should I mention it at all? The other night as I sat reading the words of the Apostle Paul, I read the following verse: "And withal they learn to be idle, wandering about from house to house; and not only idle, but tattlers also and busybodies, speaking things which they ought not" (1 Timothy 5:13).

Busybodies! That just about describes those Salem teenagers. Paul certainly doesn't mince words, does he? And the results in this case were disastrous.

May I suggest that rumor and gossip are still with us? In fact, a good friend insists that after his wife started the rumor around campus that he was going to marry her, he felt obligated to do so. However, when they're seen together, it is obvious who would have wanted to start the rumor!

A simple statement, repeated over and over, somehow doesn't sound the same as it did in the beginning. Even innocent statements can sound guilt-ridden after a few renditions. We need to be careful. As an illustration, let me share a delightful example by an unidentified person about the army. Now, for those of us who have been in the military, we will be overwhelmed with feelings of nostalgia:

"The colonel told the major—At nine o'clock tomorrow there will be an eclipse of the sun, something which does not occur every day. Get the men to fall out in the company street in their fatigues so they will see this rare phenomenon, and I will explain it to them. In case of rain we will not be able to see anything, so take the men to the gym.

"The major told the captain—By order of the colonel, tomorrow at nine o'clock there will be an eclipse of the sun. If it rains you will not be able to see it from the company street, so then, in fatigues, the eclipse of the sun will take place in the gym, something that does not occur every day.

"The captain told the lieutenant—By order of the colonel in fatigues tomorrow at nine o'clock in the

morning the inauguration of the eclipse of the sun will take place in the gym. The colonel will give the order if it should rain, something which occurs every day.

"*The lieutenant told the sergeant*—Tomorrow at nine the colonel in fatigues will eclipse the sun in the gym, as it occurs every day. If it is a nice day. If it rains, then in the company street.

"*The sergeant told the corporal*—Tomorrow at nine the eclipse of the colonel in fatigues will take place because of the sun. If it rains in the gym, something which does not take place every day, you will fall out in the company street.

"*This is what the privates understood*—Tomorrow, if it rains, it looks as if the sun will eclipse the colonel in the gym. It is a shame that this does not occur every day."

Is there a private anywhere who doesn't resonate to that last interpretation?

And interpretation is just the problem. We hear, we interpret, we repeat. Those are three words I want to mention for a brief moment: hear, interpret, repeat. We all hear and we can let it go at that if we want. Or, we can read meaning into it, perhaps meaning not intended. And finally, we can repeat it if we choose... If we choose! It is up to us. An author I have been unable to identify summed gossip up this way:

Have you ever heard of gossip town
On the shore of falsehood bay,
Where old dame rumor, with rustling gown
Is going the livelong day?

It isn't far to gossip town
For people who want to go,
The idleness train will take you down
In just an hour or so.

The thoughtless road is a popular route,
And most folks start that way
But it's steep down grade, if you don't look out
You'll land in falsehood bay.

You glide through the valley of vicious folk
And into the tunnel of hate,
Then crossing the add-to-bridge you walk
Right into the city gate.

The principal street is called they-say,
And I've heard of the public well,
And the breezes they blow from falsehood bay
Are laden with don't-you-tell!

In the midst of town is telltale park
You're never quite safe while there
For its owner is madam suspicious remark,
Who lives on the street don't care.

Just back of the park is slander's row,
'Twas there that good name died,
Pierced by a dart from jealousy's bow,
In the hands of envious pride.

From gossip town, peace long since fled,
But trouble, grief and woe,
And sorrow and care you'll meet instead
If ever you chance to go.
("Gossip Town.")

It is our choice, but we ought to remember that at the point we choose to interpret and repeat, someone's reputation may very well be on the line.

Do you remember Iago in Shakespeare's *Othello*? He put those Salem teenagers to shame. One of my platoon sergeants must have been his twin brother. Iago was the one villain in Shakespeare's plays that I loved to hate. However, he did utter one of the greatest lines ever written. Do you recall?

> Who steals my purse steals trash; 'Tis something,
>   nothing;
> 'Twas mine, 'tis his, and has been slave to
>   thousands;
> But he that filches from me my good name
> Robs me of that which not enriches him,
> And makes me poor indeed.
> (William Shakespeare, *Othello.*)

Isn't that a great statement? No wonder the Lord condemns gossip and those who use it.

For a final moment, let's flip the coin on its positive side and hear the counsel from Proverbs. Ponder carefully: "A talebearer revealeth secrets: but he that is of a faithful spirit concealeth the matter" (Proverbs 11:13). Now, that's something worth hearing, interpreting and repeating. Especially the last lines: "But he that is of a faithful spirit concealeth the matter."

How would it be if each of us were to keep silent when we heard something that shouldn't be repeated? I don't know about you, but I try to conceal my faults; and I appreciate it when others, who see them, keep them concealed. Such friends are truly "of a faithful spirit." You will notice that when you hear a rumor or gossip, and you keep it to yourself, you get an especially good feeling. The Lord is trying to tell us something.

So, with that in mind, let me give just three suggestions that will help us do a little bit better. Let's

1. Avoid listening to gossip, when practical (that is not always possible).

2. Avoid repeating any we may hear.

3. Look for occasions to say good about others.

You will find that that kind of a "faithful spirit" will rub off. Others will take your lead. You will like yourself and others much better, and they will like you, because they know they can trust you. And, finally, you will feel better about the Lord and the following words. And with his words, I bear my witness that building is always more enjoyable than tearing down; that keeping quiet is many times more satisfying than telling.

"But I say unto you, That every idle word that men shall speak, they shall give account thereof in the day of judgment.

"For by thy words thou shalt be justified, and by thy words thou shalt be condemned." (Matthew 12:36-37.)

The Outward Appearance

When you get to heaven,
You will likely view
Many folks whose presence there
Will be a shock to you.

But keep it very quiet
Do not even stare
Doubtless there'll be many folks
Surprised to see you there!

 I don't know who wrote that
clever piece of verse, but he or she had the right idea.
When I first read it I had to smile. And, at the same
time, I was forced to reflect on its deeper meaning. I
imagine that when we finally arrive in heaven, there
will be a few surprises awaiting us, including some of
those in attendance. Or, perhaps even more sobering,
those who are not.

There is a popular song sung by Johnny Mathis that is entitled "It's Not for Me to Say." I suppose that puts the whole thing in a nutshell. Wouldn't it be great if we all believed that sentiment enough to do something about it? I think we are all guilty of saying what we often attribute to mothers-in-law: "Now, it's not my place to say, but..." and away we go! We do have a tendency to judge.

Do you remember David in the Old Testament? The Prophet Samuel had been told by the Lord that King Saul was no longer acceptable to him. He was told: "I will send thee to Jesse the Bethlehemite: for I have provided me a king among his sons" (1 Samuel 16:1). Samuel was to go to the home of Jesse and anoint one of his sons to become the new king.

Well, isn't it interesting that even prophets are human? Samuel wanted to choose the wrong son, the one who *looked* like he ought to be king. His name was Eliab...tall, dark and handsome. "But the Lord said unto Samuel, Look not on his countenance, or on the height of his stature; because I have refused him: for the Lord seeth not as man seeth; for man looketh on the outward appearance, but the Lord looketh on the heart" (1 Samuel 16:7). It is reassuring to know that looks are not that important to the Lord—especially for some of us. The Lord looks at our heart.

Anyway, Samuel proceeded to interview seven of Jesse's sons, none of whom was the right man for the job. Then, finally, he asked: "Are here all thy children?" (1 Samuel 16:11.) And, of course, there was still one more, the youngest—David. And when Samuel saw David, the Lord said to the prophet, "Arise, anoint him: for this is he" (1 Samuel 16:12).

Wouldn't it be a great thing if we all had the gift of judgment—if we could look into the heart before saying or doing something to affect the life of another? Unfortunately, or perhaps fortunately, we can't. And since we can't, why don't we use as our theme the lyrics of that old favorite, "It's Not for Me to Say"? We would certainly save ourselves, and others, a lot of headaches.

Ralph Woods tells a story of someone who learned the lesson the hard way. "It seems that a prosperous Wall Street broker met, fell in love with and was frequently seen escorting about town a rising actress of gentility and dignity. He wanted to marry her, but being a cautious man he decided that before proposing matrimony he should have a private investigating agency check her background and present activities. 'After all,' he reminded himself, 'I have both a growing fortune and my reputation to protect against a marital misadventure.'

"The Wall Streeter requested that the agency was not to reveal to the investigator the identity of the client requesting the report on the actress.

"In due time the investigator's report was sent to the broker. It said the actress had an unblemished past, a spotless reputation, and her friends and associates were of the best repute. 'The only shadow,' added the report, 'is that currently she is often seen around the town in the company of a young broker of dubious business practices and principles.'" (Ralph L. Woods, *Wellsprings of Wisdom,* pp. 18-19.)

Jesus said: "Judge not, that ye be not judged. For with what judgment ye judge, ye shall be judged: and with what measure ye mete, it shall be measured to you again." (Matthew 7:1-2.)

Our broker friend certainly learned that lesson. Sometimes we learn the hard way, when it could be so much easier.

Here is another example which illustrates the point:

"A tired farmer, oppressed by the noonday heat, sat under a walnut tree for some rest, and as he sat there he looked at the pumpkin vines and said to himself, 'God is really very foolish and inexperienced; he puts heavy pumpkins on a frail vine that has so little strength it has to lie on the ground. And then he puts small walnuts on a big tree with branches that can hold a man. Any man can do better than that!'

"Just then a breeze dislodged a walnut from the tree under which the farmer sat, and the walnut fell on the critic's head. The old man rubbed his head ruefully and said, 'It's a good thing there wasn't a pumpkin up there instead of a walnut.'" (Ralph L. Woods, *Wellsprings of Wisdom*, p. 11.)

It is one thing to judge our fellowmen, but it is quite another to judge our Eternal Father. Sometimes, because of our lack of understanding we suppose that our Father has none. Or worse still, that he doesn't exist. Some of us deserve a pumpkin dropped on us from twenty feet. But, because the Lord loves us, and because he is patient, he doesn't.

Isn't there something to be learned there? If we really made up our minds, we could use our own patience and love, and stop dropping pumpkins from twenty feet, whether it is for the sake of a wife, a husband, a father or mother, brother or sister, friend or stranger. Instead of making our judgments and dropping the pumpkin on them, let's look a little deeper at others and at ourselves—not just at the "outward appearance." Hold onto that pumpkin.

I would like to challenge every one of us to do something about the habit of judging. The next time you are tempted to judge, hold off—start singing the words of Mr. Mathis's song, "It's Not for Me to Say." Because, in truth, it isn't. I bear my witness that homes will be happier, children more secure, couples more loving, friends more appreciative, and strangers more welcome.

May we understand that he who could be most severe in judgment is the most patient and understanding. May we always emulate him.

Speak as Friends

A few short years ago (at least they seemed short to me) I was privileged to play a little professional baseball. That great experience was interrupted in the early forties by a world conflict. Apparently our enemies didn't understand how important baseball could be to a struggling young pitcher. In those wonderful days of youth and sports I learned some interesting lessons. One of the most important to me was that of communication. Each player had to know exactly what his teammates were going to do in a given situation. When that communication failed, so did we. Sometimes the failure could be hilarious. One such incident appeared in *Sports Illustrated* and bears repeating. I can relate totally to that strange event.

"Before going into college basketball coaching, Dick Schultz, head coach at the University of Iowa, was a minor league baseball catcher. He once had a manager who was given to eccentric line-up changes.

"The manager decided one night to put a rookie third baseman at first base, a position he had never played before. The inevitable happened. A left-handed batter drilled a grounder to the inexperienced first baseman, who grabbed the ball and, instead of stepping on the base for the out, reflexively he began to throw, quite as if he were playing third base, but almost halfway through the throwing motion he realized where he was and fell into a series of contortions in an effort to keep from throwing the ball away. The runner was so startled by this that he stopped on the baseline. The first baseman finally fired the ball to home plate, where catcher Schultz made a startled grab.

"'I didn't want the ball,' Schultz says, 'so I threw it back to him.'

"Although the runner had stopped, the first baseman still did not think to step on first. Instead, he did what the third baseman would do. He cut him off and started a rundown play. The runner, by now as confused as anyone, fell into the act as the first baseman and Schultz began throwing the ball back and forth. Finally the runner made his break back to his last move, which happened to be home. Schultz tagged him and the umpire bellowed, 'You're out!!!'

"Schultz had only one question. He turned to the umpire and inquired innocently: 'What would you have done if he had been safe?'" (*Sports Illustrated,* April 5, 1971.)

Imagine being called out at home on a grounder to first. Now some of you women readers won't understand what happened at all. To you, baseball may seem as complicated as the man you married. But, that baseball situation is very much like trying to get a family of teenagers packed for vacation. Without superb communication, things can go haywire. I think between baseball and teenagers, I have learned some of life's greatest lessons—communication (or the lack of it) being one of the most important.

I really believe that learning to communicate with those around us is not only possible, but also not nearly as difficult as some would have us believe.

I would like to suggest a simple rule to use daily in improving our communication. As is true of all great rules, it is an eternal one suggested by the Lord. He taught it to Moses. You will remember that when Moses led the children of Israel into the wilderness from Egypt, he had occasion to communicate with the Lord. A marvelous scripture relates that happening: "And the Lord spake unto Moses face to face, as a man speaketh unto his friend" (Exodus 33:11).

That is as great a clue on communication as we could find. From it let's extract a rule of thumb: No matter with whom we communicate, let's do our best to both talk and listen as the Lord would do with us—as a friend. If we would just practice doing that every day, lines of communication would be opened that have been plugged for years. I bear solemn witness that it is a true principle.

Now, I will be the first to admit that it is not easy or automatic, but it works. The next time you speak, ask yourself, "How would the Lord say the same thing to me?" The answer is easy: "With kindness and consideration." Not with big words or flowery language, but simply and sincerely. I am reminded of a little piece of poetry by Arthur Kudner:

> Never fear big long words,
> Big words name little things.
> All big things have little names,
> Such as life and death, peace and war.
> Or dawn, day, night, hope, love, home.
> Learn to use little words in a big way.

It is hard to do but they say what you mean.

When you don't know what you mean, use big
    words.

That often fools little people.

(Arthur Kudner, "Little Words," *Saturday Review,*
April 14, 1962.)

Great advice. Let's say what we mean, but do it simply
and with kindness.

That is half the rule. Now for the other half. When
we listen, let's really pay attention—the way our
Heavenly Father does with us. Even when those
around us don't say it exactly right, we generally know
what they mean. We sometimes just like to misunderstand on purpose. But understand, we generally do. It
is very much like a few of my favorite excerpts from
letters received by a certain county welfare office.

Here is a comment of one upset welfare recipient:
"I can't get my sick pay and I got six children. Can you
tell me why?" Do you understand what she thought
she was saying?

Here's another misunderstood soul: "Sirs, I am
forwarding my marriage certificate and my two
children, one of which is a mistake as you can see." I
think we know what she *really* meant to say.

Here's a third claimant: "Please send my wife's
form to fill out." Now, although there are some
husbands who would like to do the same, that is not
what this gentleman means.

And finally: "Unless I get my husband very soon, I
will be forced to lead an immortal life." Someday she
will, but right now she means something completely
different.

In each case, I think you and I knew what the
intention was. So let's listen—really listen—and make
sure we understand what is being said.

I repeat, it is amazing what happens when that

simple rule is put into use. I know from personal experience the results.

Paul also understood the principle and its consequences. Speaking to those members of the Church in Ephesus, he gave them this excellent counsel: "Let no corrupt communication proceed out of your mouth, but that which is good to the use of edifying, that it may minister grace unto the hearers" (Ephesians 4:29).

Paul evidently knew that those words would apply to our day. If we follow the rule, we will do exactly the two things Paul wanted to have happen:

1. Our words will edify.

2. Those who hear us will receive our grace, or kindness.

Once more, here is the rule: No matter with whom we communicate, let's do our best to both talk and listen as the Lord would do with us—as a friend. Now, let's practice that! Try it for one whole day. You will be surprised! Try it for a week. You will be amazed! Try it for a year. You will be astounded! Try it for a lifetime. You will be saved in the kingdom of God. And I bear witness that in the process you will influence for good the lives of spouses, children, friends and enemies.

May we take this challenge. May we adopt this simple rule. May we learn to communicate, especially with those who depend on us.

The Human Touch

Have you ever put a puzzle together without having any idea of what it was supposed to look like? I have, and it is frustrating. However, after enough pieces are in place, all of a sudden the picture begins to take shape.

I had that experience one evening as I sat and read the New Testament. As I read, certain phrases began falling into place. They were not necessarily located close to each other, but they contained a similar pattern. A principle began to emerge in which I strongly believe. After some time I began to write phrases on a piece of paper. Let me share a few. These, in particular, refer to Jesus Christ and his mortal ministry:

"And he touched her hand, and the fever left her" (Matthew 8:15).

"Then touched he their eyes....And their eyes were opened" (Matthew 9:29-30).

"And they brought young children to him, that he should touch them" (Mark 10:13).

"And he touched his ear, and healed him" (Luke 22:51).

"He touched with his hand the disciples whom he had chosen" (3 Nephi 18:36).

Then add to these fragments the picture of John the Beloved on Christ's breast at the Last Supper.

The picture is not complete, but it is close enough to show clearly a great principle. We've all seen it demonstrated in hundreds of ways—a handshake, an arm around the waist, a pat on the back, a hug, a kiss on the cheek, and the list goes on. I guess we can call it any number of things, but I like to call it good old-fashioned affection. I believe in the human touch and so does the Lord. He touched those he healed. He touched the children. He put his hands on his apostles.

There is something about physical contact that is wonderful. It lifts, it reassures. It says "I care" in a hundred different ways.

Unfortunately, in our society, affection is sometimes misinterpreted. But it can be godly. I am grateful to those in my life who have understood the importance of touching—of affection.

I love the following story. I have used it often. It shows the power of affection, of contact between two special people.

"At one time, I was shaving, and the little prattler wanted to know what I was doing. I said, 'Shaving.'

"'What 'oo doin' t'at for?' she asked.

"I replied that I was making my face smooth, so that she could kiss me. But when I had finished, something else took my attention, and I forgot about the kiss, but she had not, and asked, archly—

"'Is 'oors face smoove *now*, papa?'

"Thus reminded, I stooped and received her kiss, but did not kiss her in return, waiting to see what she would do. She went to the other side of the room, and after a moment's pause, said in a sweet, reproachful way, '*Mine face is smoove, too, papa!*' " (*Juvenile Instructor,* March 1890, p. 157.)

Now I ask, who could resist such a plea? Unfortunately, some do. I don't understand it, but they do.

Well, it's also a given fact that not all faces are shaven; not all are handsome; not all are lovable. A friend I have likes to brag that he was so ugly as a baby that when he was born the doctor slapped his mother. I don't believe it. But ugly or not, my friend got his share of kisses and hugs and physical affection. That's one of the reasons he is so well adjusted.

The other morning on the radio I listened to the most amazing research I have heard in a long time. It was done by a German research team. It was research on how to be healthier, live longer, and earn more money. It's intended for men, but how could it work on men and not their wives? Here's the secret:

"Kiss your wife each morning when you leave for work!

"You don't have to feel like kissing her; just do it! That's the secret of success. The meticulous German researchers discovered that men who kiss their wives every morning have fewer automobile accidents on their way to work than men who omit the morning kiss. The good-morning kissers miss less work because of sickness than the non-kissers. And they earn from 20-30 percent more money and live some five years longer than men who are stingy with their kisses.

"Dr. Szabo of West Germany explains that a husband who kisses his wife every morning begins the day with a positive attitude.

"Is there any hope for those gentlemen who neglect to deliver that morning kiss? They have a lot going against them, insists Dr. Szabo. These unaffectionate fellows start the day with negative feelings and doubts about their own worth. You see, a kiss is a kind of seal of approval.

"If you have been rushing out of the house in the morning without kissing your wife, consider changing your ways. It might make a change in your wife too. Why not try it?"

I submit that most of us have always been in favor of a kiss with that special person, but I wonder how many knew we were making a financial investment at the same time. If Wall Street only knew what a great investment they were missing!

And, speaking of investments, may I suggest that there are few investments we can make in each other more important than affection. The human touch is vital to survival. As I've said before, it can and should be appropriate and good.

Paul seemed to understand this great principle as he counseled the saints in Rome. He said: "Be kindly affectioned one to another" (Romans 12:10). Good advice from a prophet of God.

Now, may I suggest that we seriously examine how we're doing in this important area of our lives. Especially, let's look at our families. Are we showing them the warmth they need? And you'll notice I used the word "need" and not "deserve." If we had to deserve the love and affection we receive, we would all be in trouble. But since that's not the criteria, why don't we concentrate on a simple daily checklist to help us do better. It can contain whatever we think appropriate, but it should help us make sure we're giving that "human touch" to our mates, our children and our parents. That hug, that kiss, that arm on the shoulder will make a tremendous difference to every member of the family—every day. And where appropriate, let's reach out to those around us. There are those who long to be recognized and appreciated by a simple touch.

Finally, may I bear fervent testimony to the truthfulness of this great principle. It is a holy principle which will go with us into eternity. And when we finally return to our heavenly home, I assure you it will be to open arms. May we practice and prepare now.

III
Your World

The Golden Door

I love America! I don't think I have ever seen the Statue of Liberty without getting a chill up my spine. Engraved on that stately lady are some words I hope will never be forgotten:

Give me your tired, your poor,
Your huddled masses yearning to breathe free,
The wretched refuse of your teeming shore,
Send these, the homeless, tempest-tost to me,
I lift my lamp beside the golden door.

Recently I received from a friend some information he thought I might enjoy. I did! So much so that I decided I wanted to share it. It caused some deep reflections, which were good for me. I think it could do us all some good. First, here is what he sent me:

"The Soviet Union has a larger population, larger territory and more resources than the United States. And they have had 50 years to put into practice a completely socialistic system. For the United States to be

able to equal the Russian way of life after 50 years we
would have to—

cut all pay checks by seventy-five percent;

move sixty million of our workers to farms;

abandon two-thirds of our steel making capacity;

tear up fourteen of every fifteen miles of highway;

do away with two-thirds of our railroad tracks;

knock down seventy percent of our housing and
move the entire population into what remains; rip
out nine of every ten telephones;

junk nineteen of every twenty automobiles;

destroy forty million televisions;

find a free enterprise country to sell us the necessary wheat to keep us going.

"Socialism—Equal   division   of   poverty.   Free
Enterprise—Unequal division of wealth." (Jay Van
Andel, "An Insight," BYU, 1979.)

Isn't that amazing? It is also astounding. I hadn't
realized how far ahead of the world we are, especially
in so many things we take for granted.

The comparison with the USSR also triggered in
my mind the story of Nila Magidoff. This great lady
was a Russian immigrant to the United States in 1948.
She had married an American news correspondent,
but they were expelled for alleged spying. The account
of her first experiences in our country are as graphic
and as inspiring as any I have ever heard. May I share
with you just a few. The first one deals with her first
night in the U.S.A. Here are her own words:

"I went to the hotel. When I arrived I gave my
document to the desk clerk. You see, I had given up
my Soviet citizenship. I was not yet an American; so I
had a temporary document. It was beautiful, with a
picture, ribbons, stamps, everything. I gave it to the
clerk to be registered. He looked and said, 'Nice
picture; sign your name.' By the movements of his

eyes I noticed that he didn't even look at my name and I told him, 'You didn't check my name! I can sign any name I want.' He said, 'Please do! But why would you sign any name but your own?' This was my first smell of freedom. In Russia, when I spent just one day out of my home, I had to register with the police.'' (From ''My Discovery of America,'' BYU, February 23, 1959.)

What a great way for her to discover the difference between this country and her own! For any who have traveled abroad, her experience is especially meaningful. For Nila, the differences between Russia and the United States were just the beginning. Let me share another with you through her own eyes as she continues:

''I left San Francisco by train the same evening for New York. The next morning I had my first American breakfast. I was in the diner car, sitting at the same table with very successful-looking businessmen. You know, the kind of businessmen who, when they pick up a menu, never look to the right. They just read to the left. When I pick up a menu, I study carefully the right and then I switch to the left. When I needed sugar for my coffee, I didn't know that in restaurants and diners they packed each piece of sugar separately. I looked around. I didn't want to ask the businessmen. Well, there was a nice, big silver gadget. I picked it up and shook its contents in my coffee. The businessmen asked me, 'I beg your pardon. Why do you put *salt* in your coffee?' I was ashamed of my mistake, but I looked straight in his eyes and said, 'You know, a very famous doctor in Russia discovered if you drink one cup of coffee with salt in the morning, you stay young and slim as long as you live!' I finished my coffee and departed. It was horrible.''

Suffice it to say that when I had finished reading her experiences, both here and in Russia, I sat and pondered and appreciated some of the little things I take for granted; even some things I don't always like, but which are all-American. While I sat there in the comfort of my den, I decided I liked traffic jams, red tape, courthouses, voting booths, the highway patrol, the stock market, disposable diapers, and paying taxes. Well, maybe that last one is somewhat liberal, but I will stick with the rest. I *do* love America!

Look again at the poem by Emma Lazarus quoted earlier—the one engraved on the Statue of Liberty. In particular, re-read the last line: "I lift my lamp beside the golden door." That is a great line, but it causes me some concern. The golden door will remain open as long as we are willing, as Americans, to hold it open. And holding open any door requires effort. As George Bernard Shaw put it: "Liberty means responsibility. That is why most men dread it."

Although Mr. Shaw's estimation of man is a little negative, he has a point. Many men fear the responsibility. But by the same token, just as many do not. I watched during the Second World War as many of my buddies gave their lives for this country. Oh, they didn't want to die—they loved life. But when it came right down to it, they did what they had to do. And because I will never forget their faces, I don't think I will ever stop being concerned.

I'll tell you what concerns me the most. It is that we will become so accustomed to the slow curtailment of our freedom that it will be gone before we notice it; it is that we'll be slowly overcome by filth and moral pollution before we can pull ourselves out. This concern is well-stated in a little prose by an author I've been unable to identify:

"There's an old story that says you can't kill a frog by dropping him into boiling water. He reacts so quickly to the sudden heat that he jumps out before he is hurt. But if you put him in cold water and then warm it up gradually, he never decides to jump until it's too late. By then he's cooked!

"Men are just as foolish. Take away their freedom overnight and you've got a violent revolution. But steal it from them gradually (under the guise of 'security,' 'peace,' or 'progress') and you can paralyze an entire generation."

Often you can feel things heating up, can't you? I know our Heavenly Father can. He is concerned about this nation—about us. He inspired great men to come here. He inspired great men to establish this nation. And he has inspired great men to lead us against those who would shut that golden door. The Lord himself declared that this land is "a choice land above all other lands, a chosen land of the Lord; wherefore the Lord would have that all men should serve him who dwell upon the face thereof" (Ether 13:2).

I love America! I have every confidence that the Lord will preserve us. But we must do our part. We must serve him. And if we need to change, we can do that too. He expects us to. This is *his* land. We are *his* children. And the commandments are *his* commandments. May we live them!

I testify that this land has a divine destiny and that we have an important part to play. May we understand that part and do it. May we, in every deed, hold open that golden door.

Lives in Crisis

An article in the newspaper caught my eye the other day because it was titled "Read and Weep." What world condition could deserve such an introduction? A very disturbing one, it seems, for the article was a listing of the latest statistics regarding teen pregnancy. Listen to these:

1. One million American teenagers become pregnant every year.

2. More than one-third of them will have abortions.

3. More than 700,000 teens gave birth in 1982. Of this number 350,000 were seventeen or under; 13,000 were under fifteen—mere children themselves.

In the past sixteen years, out-of-wedlock births to teens have more than doubled.

What are we to do about all these lives in crisis; about all the illegitimate children born to youngsters who are not ready for the role of parent, husband or wife? The answers we hear on every hand are almost as disturbing as the situation itself. Ellen Goodman, syndicated columnist, said, "Short of locking the entire teenage population in their room, the only thing adults can do is help them avoid the most permanent and disastrous of consequences—pregnancy." And the way we always hear that teenage pregnancy can be avoided is by family planning—contraception for teenagers.

Can there be any more dramatic admission of society's failure to transmit moral values to our youth than this solution to the teenage pregnancy problem? Have we become so depraved that we have forgotten or given up on the only real solution to teenage pregnancy—the old-fashioned virtue called chastity? Are we really so ready to give up on ourselves and our teenagers? From the teenagers I know it is insulting to suggest that the only way to control them is to lock them in the house or pass out contraceptives. Society has become too willing to give a mechanistic solution to what is completely a moral problem. We are only treating the symptoms of the problem instead of confronting its causes.

Eunice Kennedy Shriver, who has long worked with the problem of teenage pregnancy, noted this in the *Washington Star,* dated July 3, 1977. She said:

"Recently, I went to a center for teenage girls, where the teacher asked what they would like to discuss most. Human biology? Care for their infant? Physiology of child birth? Family planning? The girls showed no interest.

"Then the teacher asked: 'Would you like to discuss how to say no to your boyfriend without losing his love?' All hands shot up."

As Mrs. Shriver said, "Over the years I have discovered that teenagers would rather be given standards than contraceptives."

A letter dated February 8, 1979, to a well-known columnist was reproduced in the *Deseret News*. It came from a sad little girl who had never been given standards.

"Dear Abby," she began. "Today is my fifteenth birthday and I feel like forty. I developed early and thought that because I looked mature I could handle any situation. Well I was wrong.

"I started dating when I was twelve, and before I was thirteen I was going steady with a seventeen-year-old dude. I gave in to him and that's when my troubles began. He dropped me and I started going with a friend of his.

"I gave in to him too (on the first date), and from then on it was one guy after another.

"I'm not writing for advice, Abby, it's too late for that. Now I have to live down a bad reputation. (Guys talk afterwards, I found that out.) I just hope you will print this for girls who beg their mothers to let them date and go steady before they know how to handle [it].

"No matter how mature a girl thinks she is at thirteen, she's only a kid. Sign me... 'No good at fifteen.'"

What a pathetic letter! No good at fifteen! When she should have the whole world ahead of her. What are we to do for this girl and the others like her?

First, we should take a hard look at a society which on one hand refuses to support moral values like chastity for the youth and on the other hand calls teenage pregnancy one of its gravest problems. What hypocrisy! Everywhere we turn in our world today we see examples of sexual permissiveness. What are the youth to think when advertising, movies and television suggest over and over to them that sex is mere recreation, something akin to golf or tennis? What are they to think when so many of their idols, the movie stars and singers of the day, flaunt a lifestyle that includes open living arrangements, divorces and abortions? These, of course, are all reported to us as casually as the weather.

Next, as parents, we need to consider what we have taught our children about sex, commitment and responsibility. Too many good parents who ought to know better avoid that topic with their children, thinking it too delicate or embarrassing to discuss. But, parents, if we do not discuss this area with our children they will hear about it from someone else, perhaps with its moral and spiritual dimensions completely left out. If we do not tell them that sex and reproduction is one of the Lord's most sacred gifts to us, to be confined strictly to the marriage relationship, they may not ever hear it from anyone else. As Mrs. Shriver said, "To refuse to discuss the values that pervade [the] sexual relationship is to teach young people that this important human experience is not a matter for moral reflection and discourse."

We need to teach our children standards. We need to be unafraid to stick by some rules in our homes, waiting until they are at least sixteen for that first date, armed with self-control and moral values transmitted to them by their parents.

And finally, we need to understand that often sexually active youngsters are searching for the love and warmth in a human relationship, however fleeting, that they are not getting at home. Families where there is no communication between parent and child—families torn apart by social and economic pressures—are often the families that produce this kind of child. When a child is insecure or suffers from low self-esteem, he may look somewhere other than his family for the love he lacks. To ensure our children against this, let's keep the channels of communication open. Let's take time for them. Talk to them! Give them the warmth that every human being needs, especially when they are in the traumatic teenage years.

The only control worthy of consideration with regard to the teenage pregnancy problem is self-control. It is the oldest solution in the world to what seems to be a terribly modern problem, but it is the only one that works—that treats causes and not just symptoms. May we have the intelligence to know the difference.

Who's Who

I am reminded of a book which some hold to be almost sacred. It is called *Who's Who in America.* I have seen it on the shelves in libraries and in the homes and offices of those whose names appear therein. I even have several copies. If your name is in *Who's Who* you are supposedly well on your way.

Then, just the other day, a friend of mine pointed with some pride to a *Who's Who in American High Schools.* His son's picture and vita were included in its hallowed pages. Then, added to the two volumes already mentioned is another, *Who's Who in American Colleges and Universities.* It also contains the names of those who have excelled in their respective fields.

Although I speak somewhat lightly of these three volumes and others like them, I sincerely compliment those whose names are included. It takes effort and accomplishment to be so honored. It is a witness, to any who care to read, that there are individuals who are willing to pay the price of excellence. It is a privilege to find your name in one of these books.

There is another book I have been thinking about lately which is even more prestigious than the ones I have already mentioned. It is a book upon whose pages we should all find our names. In fact, this can be a reality if we desire it. I suppose it is on my mind because I studied it again the other night. This is what I read:

"And I saw the dead, small and great, stand before God; and the books were opened: and another book was opened, which is the book of life: and the dead were judged out of those things which were written in the books, according to their works.

"And the sea gave up the dead which were in it; and death and hell delivered up the dead which were in them: and they were judged every man according to their works." (Revelation 20:12-13.)

Now, that is what I call a *Who's Who!* We will all be judged out of the records kept for this earth, but only the righteous will be found in the Lamb's book of life. If we can get into the *Who's Who in Heaven* we will be all right.

I submit that getting into the Lord's *Who's Who* is possible for us all. It takes effort, but can you imagine how we will feel when we stand before our Father in Heaven and find our names written in his book? It surely beats the alternative!

One problem I have noticed with our modern world is the skepticism toward that possibility. Some, especially the young, say: "Who, me?" And their elders often feel the same.

Let me suggest a few things we can do *right now* to start making sure our names are on the Lord's list. They are simple things, but then, most things that are really important are just that. The first suggestion comes from the great Prophet Alma.

"And now I say unto you, all you that are desirous to follow the voice of the good shepherd, come ye out from the wicked, and be ye separate, and touch not their unclean things;...

"For the names of the righteous shall be written in the book of life, and unto them will I grant an inheritance at my right hand." (Alma 5:57-58.)

Alma hits it right on the head. We must first have a desire to follow the Lord. How is your desire? How is mine? Do we *really* want to follow him? If you don't have a desire, kneel down and ask him to give you one. He will! He has promised to do so.

Once we have a desire, the prophet counsels us, "Come...out from the wicked." That is what happens when we have a real desire to follow the Savior. It is easier said than done, but it is possible. He has promised that too.

Now, how do we do that? How do we "come...out from the wicked"? I believe it is as simple as we make it. Whatever we are involved in that is not right, let's stop doing it. There are good people around us who will help if we ask. And the Lord will help us when no one else can. And what do we stop? Well, for starters how about drugs, or alcohol, or immorality, or filthy language, or dishonesty, or gossip, or whatever is in the way? It can be done! Deciding to do it is a critical step. The desire to do so is a must. Then with that desire, and with our lives getting better a little bit at a time, there is something else we can do to help secure our names in the Lord's *Who's Who.* Do you remember the man who found out for himself?

Abou Ben Adhem

Abou Ben Adhem (may his tribe increase!)
Awoke one night from a deep dream of peace,
And saw, within the moonlight in his room,

Making it rich, and like a lily in bloom,
An angel writing in a book of gold:

Exceeding peace had made Ben Adhem bold,
And to the presence in the room he said,
"What writest thou?" The vision raised its head,
And with a look made of all sweet accord
Answered, "The names of those who love the
    Lord."
"And is mine one?" said Abou. "Nay, not so,"
Replied the angel. Abou spoke more low,
But cheerily still, and said, "I pray thee, then,
Write me as one that loves his fellow men."

The angel wrote, and vanished. The next night
It came again with a great wakening light,
And showed the names whom love of God had
    blessed,
And, lo, Ben Adhem's name led all the rest!
(Leigh Hunt.)

Well, how are we doing in that area? I have found consistently in my life that those who are trying daily to put their lives in order instinctively want to reach out to those around them. The more Christlike they become the more they act like Christ. Now, I'm not talking about perfect people. I'm talking about kids and teenagers and moms and dads—you and me. Common people do uncommon things when they love the Lord.

And now, for the final question: Where do we start? Well, how about in our personal lives and in our own homes. Teenagers, reach out to your folks, even when they aren't easy to love. And parents, take some time with your children. How about brothers and sisters trying harder to get along? How about neighbors doing things *for* each other (instead of *to* each other)? How about simple acts of kindness to those we love, or should love. It makes a difference. It really does. And before we know it, like Abou Ben Adhem, we'll find our names in the most important book ever compiled.

I would like you to know that from experience I know these things are true. They work! I also am sure that a loving Father in Heaven delights to put our names in his book. What good father doesn't want the best for his children? And finally, I give you my witness that there is, in reality, a book of life. And it is possible for every soul to be a part of that sacred volume. Let us begin, or continue, as the case may be, and we will eventually be so rewarded.

Boomerangs

Souvenirs are great! I have my share of tourist favorites—a vase from Taiwan, onyx from Mexico, dishes from Denmark, silk from Korea, wood from Tahiti, stones from Brazil, and on and on. However, one of the most interesting I have is a boomerang from Australia. We all know their function. Throw them away and they will come flying right back.

It was exactly this souvenir that came to mind one day when a friend shared a clever verse with me. It changed my concept of a boomerang, and it may change yours. Allow me to share it.

> When a bit of sunshine hits ye,
>   After passing of a cloud,
> When a fit of laughter gets ye,
>   And your spine is feelin' proud,
> Don't forget to up and fling it
>   At a soul that's feelin' blue,

For the minit that ye sling it,
It's a boomerang to you.

I don't know the author, Jack Crawford, but he knows people. And, from what I can tell, he knows one of the secrets of being happy in life—sharing kindness. I am convinced you cannot give kindness away, because it somehow manages to come right back. All we can do is share it.

And besides, sharing kindness is a great deterrent to heart attacks. There is no better exercise for the heart than reaching down and lifting someone up. The Apostle Peter understood this principle and did something about it—literally. You will remember the experience of Peter and John with the lame man in Jerusalem. Having been asked for alms, Peter extended the kindest gift possible:

"Then Peter said, Silver and gold have I none; but such as I have give I thee: In the name of Jesus Christ of Nazareth rise up and walk.

"And he took him by the right hand, and lifted him up: and immediately his feet and ankle bones received strength." (Acts 3:6-7.)

Although we cannot all heal, we can all lift. We can understand. Let me illustrate with a story whose author I don't know.

"A man was putting up a sign, 'Puppies For Sale' and before he had driven the last nail, there was a small boy standing at his side. That kind of sign seems to attract small boys. The youngster wanted to know how much the puppies were going to cost. The man told him they were very good dogs and that he did not expect to let any of them go for less than $35 or $50. There was a look of disappointment, and then a question: 'I've got $2.37. Could I look at them?'

"The man whistled and called 'Lady!'—and out of

the kennel and down the runway came Lady, followed by four or five little balls of fur, with one lagging considerably behind. The boy spotted the laggard and, pointing, asked, 'What's wrong with him?' The reply was that the veterinarian had said there was no hip socket in the right hip and that the dog would always be lame. The boy's immediate rejoinder was, 'That's the one I want to buy. I'll give you $2.37 down and fifty cents a month till I get him paid for.' The man smiled and shook his head. 'That's not the dog you want. That dog will never be able to run and jump and play with you.'

"The boy, very matter-of-factly, pulled up his little trouser leg and revealed a brace running down both sides of his badly twisted right leg and under the foot, with a leather cap over the knee. 'I don't run so well myself,' he said, 'and he'll need somebody that understands him.'"

You who have small children or dogs will appreciate the kindness that both of them displayed; and, as a matter of fact, it takes a good portion of kindness on the parent's part to patiently endure puppies (and, on occasion, kids). The child of a friend of mine just got a puppy and has been sleeping with it in the doghouse to keep the puppy from whining. I consider that an act of kindness far beyond the call of duty. I understand the neighbors have another word for it!

On a more serious note, may I suggest that we come to be truly concerned for others, to be truly kind, when we understand where we stand with the Lord. It is sobering to realize how much we do (and will) depend on him for his kindness to us. If it were not for his goodness, you and I would be in deep trouble—everlasting trouble. But once we realize our relationship to him, wonderful things can happen. Please note:

I had walked life's way with an easy tread,
Had followed where comfort and pleasures led.
Until one day in a quiet place,
I met the master face to face.

With station and rank and wealth for my goal,
Much thought for my body, but none for my soul,
I had entered to win in life's mad race,
When I met the master face to face.

I met him and knew him and blushed to see
That his eyes full of sorrow were fixed on me;
And I faltered and fell at his feet that day,
While my castles melted and vanished away.

Melted and vanished, and in their place
Naught else did I see but the master's face.
And I cried aloud, "Oh, make me meet
To follow the steps of thy wounded feet."

My thought is now for the souls of men,
I have lost my life to find it again,
E'er since one day in a quiet place
I met the master face to face.

      ("I Met The Master." Authorship unknown.)

That is the starting place—with our recognition of him. It leads naturally to our next point, and it is also a sobering one: There is only one way that our Father can extend his kindness to his children—through us! If we don't do it, who will? We are all he has. But, we can do it! Being kind is one of the finest things we can do. It is also one of the easiest, because its reward is almost immediate—like a boomerang. If you don't believe me then try it! Especially on someone who is not expecting it. If being kind doesn't bring you a great feeling, nothing ever will.

May I suggest that we begin our improvement in this critical area of kindness right away—today. We cannot change yesterday, and tomorrow is too far away. Today is the day! Allow me to share the importance of that thought with this great piece of poetry. It says it perfectly:

> The bread that bringeth strength I want to give,
> The water pure that bids the thirsty live;
> I want to help the fainting day by day;
> I'm sure I shall not pass again this way.
>
> I want to give the oil of joy for tears,
> The faith to conquer crowding doubts and fears,
> Beauty for ashes may I give always;
> I'm sure I shall not pass again this way.
>
> I want to give good measure running o'er
> And into angry hearts I want to pour
> The answer soft that turneth wrath away;
> I'm sure I shall not pass again this way.
>
> I want to give to others hope and faith;
> I want to do all that the Master saith;
> I want to live aright from day to day;
> I'm sure I shall not pass again this way.
>   (Ellen H. Underwood,
>   "I Shall Not Pass Again This Way.")

With that thought, remember that kindness brings eternal rewards as well as immediate satisfaction. And since that is true, why not start in our own homes, with the most important people we know.

Go-Givers

I often hear an expression we have come to accept as commonplace — "Isn't he a go-getter?" I smile because I have used that expression myself.

As I have had time to ponder that expression, I decided there is something misleading about it. As much as we need go-getters in this world, and as helpful as they are, we need something else much more. So, to rectify the situation, I have coined a new phrase. I doubt if it will ever catch on but, nevertheless, it is worth a try. More than go-getters, we need "go-givers."

A little homey perhaps, but that new phrase is exactly what we need. Or, better still, *people* who are go-givers are exactly what we need.

A newspaper account carried an interesting incident of just such a person. A go-getter is always noticed, but often go-givers are not obvious at all.

"The District of Columbia police auctioned off about 100 unclaimed bicycles. 'One dollar,' said an eleven-year-old boy as the bidding opened on the first bike. The bidding, however, went much higher. 'One dollar,' the boy repeated hopefully each time another bike came up.

"The auctioneer, who has been auctioning stolen or lost bikes for 45 years, noticed that the boy's hopes seemed to soar highest whenever a racer was put up.

"There was one racer left. Then the bidding mounted to $8.00. 'Sold to that boy over there for $9.00,' said the auctioneer. He took $8.00 from his own pocket and asked the boy for his dollar. The youngster turned it over—in pennies, nickels, dimes and quarters—took his bike and started to leave. But he went only a few feet. Carefully parking his new possession, he went back, gratefully threw his arms around the auctioneer's neck, and cried."

Now, that is what I call a go-giver. We will probably never know the name of that man, but I assure you his name is recorded.

A great Apostle, Elder Matthew Cowley, tells of another go-giver. He relates: "I was in Canada one day about five years ago. And I went to a home of a bishop for dinner. He wanted me to stay at his home, but he didn't have room. Well, I went to dinner. When the dinner was all set he went into a little room and carried out a little woman—a lovely little soul, with white hair—and he took her over and placed her down gently in a chair at the table. Then he took a napkin and put it around her neck, pushed the chair up close. And then he went back to the room and came out with his arms around an elderly man—a little white-haired man—and then he took him over and gently placed him at the side of the woman. Then he took a napkin and put it around his neck. And then we all sat down.

"And then he said, 'Brother Cowley, this is the reason we don't have room for you. These are the parents of my wife, and we're trying to get even with them, while they're so helpless, for what they did for my wife when she was a helpless child.' And before that man and his wife took a spoonful of food, they fed the lovely parents, who couldn't feed themselves." (Matthew Cowley, Leadership Week Lectures, June 19, 1953, p. 4.)

The world is full of them, but we can use more, many more.

> "For I was an hungred, and ye gave me meat:
> I was thirsty, and ye gave me drink:
> I was a stranger, and ye took me in:
> Naked, and ye clothed me:
> I was sick, and ye visited me:
> I was in prison, and ye came unto me."
>
> (Matthew 25:35-36.)

That statement by the Lord pretty well sums up what it takes to become a go-giver. You can recognize one every time. In fact, they sometimes work side by side with those who are not. Let me illustrate.

A young man worked as an attendant at a state mental hospital. His ward was one for patients who had both mental and physical ailments. Here is an incident he was involved in.

"One night about a dozen years ago, he walked onto the ward to report for work. Just as he locked the door, a husky voice from inside a heavy wire screen called to him.

"That voice belonged to a man who was as thin as a thermometer. He was a suspected tuberculosis case. Attendants were not supposed to go near him unless they wore face masks. His face was covered with a shaggy beard, and he had a rattly cough. He sounded worse than ever when he called to the attendant.

" 'Could you put on your mask and talk to me for a minute?'

" 'Why?'

" 'Because I'm lonely,' rasped the thin little man.

" 'Sorry,' the young man lied, 'but I have to go fold the linen.'

"The attendant walked to the ward office and greeted Mrs. Della Badham, a hearty, grandmother-type who commuted every evening to work at the hospital. Then the young attendant picked up the patient checklist and strode to the far end of the ward to begin the head count. Before he was halfway through with that task, he heard a strange sound. Somebody was singing. A woman.

"He listened for a moment, then a half-smile of recognition crossed his face. That was Della's voice. Then the cocky young attendant frowned. If Della didn't cut that out, she would wake all the patients.

"Quickly, the young attendant followed the sound of her voice and found himself looking through a wire screen into the room occupied by the TB suspect. Della was seated by the man's bed, and she had her arms around the man's scrawny shoulders. He wasn't coughing any more. Della looked at him and cut her song short.

" 'He's dead,' she said.

" 'Tell me something, Della,' the young attendant said. 'How could you go in there and put your arms around that repulsive old man and sing to him like that?'

" 'Because he asked me to,' said Della. 'He was alone and afraid. I knew he was dying. I couldn't refuse a man's last request, could I?' " (From "Steve Hale's People.")

I suppose it can be difficult at times to be a go-giver, but I submit that, generally, it is much easier to be one than it is not to be one. In fact, I suggest that the key was recognized in Edwin Markham's famous verse:

> He drew a circle that shut me out—
> Heretic, rebel, a thing to flout.
> But love and I had the wit to win:
> We drew a circle that took him in.
>
> (Edwin Markham, "Outwitted.")

That is the key.

What a great world this would be if we would just start drawing our circles a little larger. We don't need to accomplish it in a day, but *today* is the time to start. How would it be if we started with our own families first: husbands, wives, mothers, fathers, brothers, sisters. Then branch out: friends, neighbors, relatives. Then enlarge the circle: acquaintances, strangers and finally, enemies. Imagine—enemies!

To be a go-giver is eternally worth it. Try it; it surely beats the alternative. I have tried it and can testify it works. You try it and your testimony of it will be the same.

Don't expect always to be praised. Don't expect always to be appreciated. Don't expect anything at all—and you will get *everything.* You will get a feeling that comes in no other way. It is a feeling born of him who gave the most. May we try it and see. But let's give it a fair shake. Be consistent for a while and the results will be amazing.

I bear you my witness that it is true and because it is true, great happiness will come to those who practice it right now. And, equally important, when it is all over, we will hear these everlastingly joyful words:

"Come, ye blessed of my Father, inherit the kingdom prepared for you from the foundation of the world:...

"Verily I say unto you, Inasmuch as ye have done it unto one of the least of these my brethren, ye have done it unto me." (Matthew 25:34, 40.)

May we all become, truly, "go-givers."

Unbreakable Truth

If you have ever attended a Sunday School class for children, you will notice that often the kids are given stars on their foreheads to denote their good behavior. Let me share a true story of one such little girl, Mitzi.

"One beautiful Sunday this cute little gal came bouncing out of Junior Sunday School class, all curls and ruffles, with a gold star pasted to her forehead. Thinking how sweet she must have been in order to receive such recognition, an adult friend asked how she got the star. Matter-of-factly, she replied, 'I stole it!' " (Margaret J. Fischer, *Ensign.*)

Ask a child an honest question and you get an honest answer. Now, Mitzi's response is typical of small children. They simply tell it like it is—not necessarily with tact—but straight out, honest-to-goodness truth. If what you want to hear is a watered-down, sugar-coated version of the truth, then don't ask a child.

Isaiah understood full well what he was saying when he prophesied: "And a little child shall lead them" (Isaiah 11:6).

Children have that great ability to take you by the hand and tell you what you need to hear.

While attending a stake conference I remember hearing a little four-year-old pray: "Heavenly Father, please bless President Kimball and all of his impossibles."

But, have you noticed that as we start growing up and as we become more "sophisticated," it is even more easy to cast aside that childlike honesty. Truth can then be sacrified on the altar of expediency with words like, "It's really not that important," or "It's kind of this way," or "Who'll know the difference anyway?" That is the temptation. But truth is truth, and when we don't have it or don't use it, the results can be dramatic, if not disastrous.

Have you heard the parable of the walrus? In particular it is about Basil. Basil was second in command in a herd. He had to report to "the old man" (the senior walrus). By the way, the old man didn't like bad news, so Basil was constantly challenged to give him the real facts. We all know that is hard to do when they are not wanted. Anyway, on one occasion...

"A new herd of walruses moved in down the beach, and with the supply of herring dwindling, this invasion could have been dangerous. No one wanted to tell the old man, though only he could take the steps necessary to meet this new competition.

"Reluctantly Basil approached the big walrus, who was still sunning himself on the large rock. After some small talk, he said, 'Oh, by the way, chief, a new herd of walruses seems to have moved into our territory.' The old man's eyes snapped open, and he filled his great lungs in preparation for a mighty bellow. But

Basil added quickly, 'Of course, we don't anticipate any trouble. They don't look like herring-eaters to me—more likely interested in minnows. And as you know, we don't bother with minnows ourselves.'

"The old man let out the air with a long sigh. 'Good! Good!' he said. 'No point in getting excited over nothing, then, is there?'

"Things didn't get any better in the weeks that followed. One day, peering down from the large rock, the old man noticed that part of his herd seemed to be missing. Summoning Basil, he grunted peevishly, 'What's going on, Basil? Where is everybody?'

"Poor Basil didn't have the courage to tell the old man that many of the younger walruses were leaving every day to join the new herd. Clearing his throat nervously, he said, 'Well chief, we've been tightening things up a bit. You know, getting rid of some of the dead wood. After all, a herd is only as good as the walruses in it.'

"'Run a tight ship, I always say,' the old man grunted. 'Glad to hear that everything's going so well.'

"Before long, everyone but Basil had left to join the new herd, and Basil realized that the time had come to tell the old man the facts. Terrified but determined, he flopped up to the large rock. 'Chief,' he said, 'I have bad news. The rest of the herd has left you.'

"The old walrus was so astonished that he couldn't even work up a good bellow. 'Left me?' he cried. 'All of them? But why? How could this happen?'

"Basil didn't have the heart to tell him so he merely shrugged helplessly.

"'I can't understand it,' the old walrus said, 'and just when everything was going so well!'" (*Management Review*, October 1961.)

This story has several lessons we can learn, but may I suggest that the most important idea concerns truth. Somehow, in difficult situations it's easier to bury truth than face it.

Oliver Wendell Holmes said: "Truth is tough. It will not break like a bubble, at a touch." (*The Professor of the Breakfast Table.*)

Truth is not the problem — we are. The truth isn't afraid of us, it's more often vice versa. But in the end, truth is our friend and chief ally. Without it, we live in ignorance. With it, we can do what Jesus indicated to his disciples: "And ye shall know the truth, and the truth shall make you free" (John 8:32). We can be free! What a great blessing!

Pilate asked the Savior a profound question while trying to determine the Lord's guilt or innocence.

"Pilate therefore said unto him, Art thou a king then? Jesus answered, Thou sayest that I am a king. To this end was I born, and for this cause came I into the world, that I should bear witness unto the truth. Every one that is of the truth heareth my voice.

"Pilate saith unto him, What is truth? And when he had said this, he went out again unto the Jews." (John 18:37-38.)

Now, isn't that something? Pilate asked the right question, "What is truth?" But then before Christ could answer, he turned his back and walked out. I wonder how many men have done the same thing when faced with an opportunity to learn truth. I love the statement of Winston Churchill: "Men occasionally stumble over the truth, but most of them pick themselves up and hurry off as if nothing had happened."

Such was the case with Pilate, and such is the case with many. But I have more confidence in us. I believe that we really *want* to come to know the truth. It won't break. And neither will we if we accept it when we find it. The more we learn and accept truth, the happier we will be. Our Heavenly Father has all truth, and the more you and I learn it, the closer we move to him. And such upward movement always brings great, personal joy.

May we seek the truth and accept it from whatever source, especially the eternal truths that will free us from spiritual ignorance. The Apostle James gave us this counsel: "If any of you lack wisdom, let him ask of God, that giveth to all men liberally, and upbraideth not; and it shall be given him" (James 1:5).

I leave you my witness that truth is knowledge. May we be humble in our honest reach for it. And when it comes knocking at our door, may we not fight against it. The truth won't break.

I pray that we may, above all else, seek and find a knowledge of the gospel of Jesus Christ. It is true. It is truth. Of that I am sure.

Age Before Beauty

Do you know how you can tell when you're getting old? I suppose there are many signs of age, but let me share with you some of the most interesting. You know you're growing old:

When you get winded while brushing your teeth.

When the only way you can get men to fall at your feet is by gluing a hundred dollar bill to each of your shoes.

When, after you get it all together, you realize you'd do better if you took it all apart.

When the first time you act your age your spouse calls an ambulance.

When your appendectomy scar hits your knee.

When a fortune-teller reads the lines around your eyes.

When the doctor who lifted your face gets a hernia.

When your crow's-feet need orthopedic shoes.

When you reach the age when you know all the answers, but no one ever bothers to ask the questions.

When the bones on your x-rays come out yellowed.

When instead of Max Factor you use straight Kemtone.

When your circulation becomes so shot that when you cross your legs, your arms to to sleep.

When you sit in a rocking chair and can't get it going.

When you get out of the shower and you're glad the mirror is fogged up.

When you get up in the morning and you have got one shoe on and one shoe off and you can't remember whether you are getting up or going to bed.

Despite our best plans and efforts, growing old is going to happen to most of us—that is, if we don't die first. But I want to mention some things about age which may be helpful.

On a more serious note, there is nothing quite so sobering as visiting a nursing home, or spending some time with a widow or widower who sits at home and waits out his days. After returning from such a trip once, I was reminded of an "Ann Landers" clipping I had collected long ago. I pulled it out that same evening and re-read it. Let me share it with you.

"Dear Ann:

"I have never written to you before, but I believe the following might interest you and your readers. I found it in an old magazine. No author's name was mentioned, just 'a heavy-hearted observer.'

" 'Yesterday was an old man's birthday. He was 91. He awakened earlier than usual, bathed, shaved and put on his best clothes. Surely they would come today, he thought.

" 'He didn't take his daily walk to the gas station to visit with the old-timers of the community, because he wanted to be right there when they came.

" 'He sat on the front porch with a clear view of the road so he could see them coming. Surely they would come today.

" 'He decided to skip his noon nap because he wanted to be up when they came.

" 'He has six children.

" 'Two of his daughters and their married children live within four miles. They hadn't been to see him for such a long time. But today was his birthday. Surely they would come today.

" 'At suppertime he refused to cut the cake and asked that the ice cream be left in the freezer. He wanted to wait and have dessert with them when they came.

" 'About 9 o'clock he went to his room and got ready for bed. His last words before turning out the lights were, "Promise to wake me up when they come."

" 'It was his birthday and he was 91.' "

Now, if that doesn't touch you, very little will.

In our modern world of sophistication and progress, I find it disturbing that the old expression "age before beauty" seems to have been reversed. Never before has there been so much emphasis on beauty and youth. And although our computer-age technology has been unsurpassed at lengthening and enriching the lives of our older citizens, I'm not so sure it has replaced or improved upon the personal touch. But, I believe there is a way we can ensure that the personal touch is never lost. The following are three bits of Old Testament counsel from the Lord. Let's see if we can use these to bless the lives of our older friends and neighbors.

First, from Proverbs: "The glory of young men is their strength: and the beauty of old men is the gray head" (Proverbs 20:29).

Second, from Job: "With the ancient is wisdom; and in length of days understanding. With him is wisdom and strength, he hath counsel and under-standing." (Job 12:12-13.)

And third, in Psalms: "Cast me not off in the time of old age; forsake me not when my strength faileth" (Psalm 71:9).

Now, from those great scriptures, let's draw three important conclusions:

1. There are advantages to old age.

2. We can learn from the wisdom and understanding of age.

3. Older folks want to be useful, not put on a shelf.

To those who wonder if we have an obligation to bring these conclusions to pass, the Lord's answer to Cain's question, "Am I my brother's keeper?" is a resounding *yes*—"Thou shalt love thy neighbour as thyself." (Genesis 4:9 and Matthew 22:39.)

The final question ought to be, "How are we going to accomplish this?" It seems to me that it shouldn't be hard to find places to start. With older friends and opportunities all around, let's—

1. Seek their counsel.

2. Visit them regularly.

3. Include them in our activities.

4. Let them share their experiences with us.

5. See to it that they have the basic necessities of life.

6. Care for them when sick.

7. Treat them as dignified human beings, not charity cases.

And the list goes on and on.

I am convinced that the more we go out of our way to help the aged, whether parents, family, friends or strangers, the more Christlike we become.

May we remember that these principles are true. Let's take advantage of the blessing of having grandpas and grandmas, fathers and mothers, friends and neighbors all around us. May we reach out to them—not with pity, but with love. I promise that as we do, we'll realize a joy never before experienced. Finally, may we do unto the aged what we will want to have done to us. Our turn is coming.

Our Todays—
Your Tomorrows

Memorial Day is somehow a day for memories, for thinking back on people who have touched your life and then passed out of it like yesterday's sunset. But their warmth lingers on. There is one such person who comes to my mind. He was my foxhole buddy in the Pacific in World War II, and a braver man I never met. He was only nineteen, and small in stature. I suppose he wouldn't have been that hard to knock over, but he had more courage and determination than the biggest, brawniest, muscle-bound soldier out there.

Now, the fighting in the Pacific was rarely direct combat. Instead we found ourselves day after day hacking through the densest jungle, wondering just where the enemy was. They were clever. They'd tie themselves under the leaves in palm trees; they'd hollow out banana plants, climb inside and be concealed within the dense growth. And you never knew quite where they were—that was until your buddy in front of you or behind you was suddenly pierced with a bayonet or sword. The men were edgy when they were assigned that kind of patrol duty. They knew only half of them would come back. But my friend had a way of acting nonchalant about it all. When he led a patrol, all the men had a resurgence of courage. Me included.

Well, we were foxhole buddies through five of the toughest campaigns in the war. Do you know what that means? Because the enemy didn't actively fight us during the daylight, the night was nothing but harassment and terror. Each evening at dusk, we American soldiers dug into foxholes in a large circle, a perimeter, to try and protect ourselves against the raids and artillery fire that erupted all around us. The rule was a simple one for us. After the sun set we could not get above ground level, no matter what the pain, or discomfort, or emergency might be. Anything above the ground level was considered the enemy and was immediately shot.

We had to live by that rule, for the enemy continually sneaked in upon us in ones and twos with knives ready to slit our throats or grenades ready to throw in our holes. On coral islands we couldn't dig down very far so we had to lie flat almost without breathing through the long, miserable nights. I remember lying there with the heaviest tropical rain filling up my hole, so sick with dingy fever I didn't know if I could stand it till morning. I remember rats two feet long jumping in upon us in those foxholes, and we couldn't move, and we couldn't yell. We just had to quietly deal with them.

But worst of all were the artillery and mortar attacks, killing men all around us and wounding others. Then through the long nights we heard American voices calling out in the most plaintive tones, "Help me; oh, help me!" And we wouldn't do anything about it because we couldn't move out of our foxholes without getting killed ourselves.

Yes, my friend and I shared all that for many battles. And his spirit and his faith never let down. And when the hard K rations and the thirst and the fear got to be too much, he was always there for me.

Finally, when we were in Okinawa, the casualties had been so high that we could no longer put two men to a foxhole. We had to spread the men out just to make a big enough circle. One night, as was the custom, the enemy was harassing our lines with mortar shells, and my friend got hit. I could hear his yell from the foxhole next to mine. I started to call out words of comfort and encouragement to him from my hole and continued to do so all night long until I was almost hoarse with the effort. "C'mon, hold on. Just a few more hours until daylight. You can make it. You have to make it. C'mon, you can do it." And he would answer very faintly.

When the first light of dawn came, I scrambled out of my hole, which was filled with a cold tropical rain, and hurried over to him. I picked him up, trying to cradle his head in my arms, and I could see he was badly hurt.

"Paul, will you do two things for me?" he said. "Will you get word to my mother that I was true to her teachings right to the end. And—if you ever have an opportunity to speak to the youth, will you tell them that it was a pleasure to lay down my life for this great country."

He died there in my arms, and later when we counted, we found over fifty shrapnel wounds on his tortured body.

He was buried in a makeshift cemetery in

Okinawa. And very fittingly it says over the arch leading to his resting place, "We gave our todays in order that you might have your tomorrows."

The question has haunted me since that time—for my friend and for all the others like him who have given their lives for a great cause, for the well-being of other generations—what are we doing with our tomorrows? Are we so swallowed up with selfishness and apathy that we are saying, in fact, your sacrifice means nothing?

It is very popular today to complain about our society, our country. Some of the complaints may be justifiable. One senator asked his constituents to give their answers on what were the worst, most senseless regulations imposed by the federal government. And did he get an earful!

Nine parents in Dallas protested against a proposed Agriculture Department regulation that would restrict the sale of junk food at public schools. As one parent said, "How dare Washington assume they have the right to say if my daughter can buy a candy bar at school." Others complained about federal paperwork, the complexity of tax forms. One Grapevine, Texas, citizen protested that the government, in order to discourage sexism in high school athletics, "insisted that boys at Grapevine High School be encouraged to become cheerleaders and that the cheerleaders should yell at as many girls' athletic activities as at boys' games regardless of whether the cheerleaders, the athletes or the coaching staff wanted them to."

The complaints go on and on. And we all have them—one kind or another. We say, "Why don't *they* do something about this. Why don't *they* do something about that? *They've* ruined the schools. *They've* increased taxes." They! They! They!

What we all must remember is this. In a free country, a democratic country, the kind my friend fought and died for, the power is with the people, and the responsibility. If you have a dream, or a complaint, you have the power to do something about it. This society can only be yours if you decide to make an impact on it; to grab your todays and tomorrows and make something of them. As one thinker once noted, "We survive because of six inches of topsoil, and the cooperation of one another." Let us not pull away from our high responsibility—full citizenship in this wonderful country. Let us not leave the responsibility, the decisions, to someone else because we were too lazy. Thousands who have made the supreme sacrifice are counting on you and me.

IV
Your Values

Filling the Reserve Tank

I enjoy resting. In fact, there are few things I enjoy more. I believe most people will relate with my feelings. It is not that I am lazy (except when it comes to my wife's "honey-do" day-off list—you know, "honey, do this," and "honey, do that"). It is just that life is hectic and rushed. I sometimes find myself with a half-day's schedule left and only a quarter of a tank of energy remaining. But, like many, I somehow find the knob to the reserve tank and make it through the day.

It is about this reserve tank I wish to talk in this chapter. On life's journey, I have found that to refuel each morning is critical. Morning personal and family prayer, together with scripture study, somehow seems to replenish the main source of daily energy. But if it weren't for that reserve tank late in the day, or at the end of the week, I wouldn't make it. I bear testimony that none of us would. We need added help.

May I suggest that the refueling of our reserve tank takes place on Sunday. It can't be done on any other day—not Monday through Friday, or even on Saturday. It must be done on the Sabbath. There is only one station available to refuel and that is the Lord's station. Unlike any other station, it is closed every day except Sunday.

I am not sure I understand all the reasons for this amazing reality, but I do know that when we keep the Sabbath day holy, our reserve tanks are filled for the coming week. We then have a right to blessings and abilities that we otherwise would not have.

There are those, however, who wish to close the Lord's Sabbath station. They don't believe what I have said, nor do they believe the Lord's command; or, at least if they do, they are not willing to make the effort to see if the station is really open. It is!

From Sinai the Lord left little doubt about the seriousness of his offer:

"Remember the sabbath day, to keep it holy.

"Six days shalt thou labour, and do all thy work.

"But the seventh day is the sabbath of the Lord thy God: in it thou shalt not do any work, thou, nor thy son, nor thy daughter, thy manservant, nor thy maidservant, nor thy cattle, nor thy stranger that is within thy gates:

"For in six days the Lord made heaven and earth, the sea, and all that in them is, and rested the seventh day: wherefore the Lord blessed the sabbath day, and hallowed it." (Exodus 20:8-11.)

The Lord has been serious about the Sabbath from the beginning. He himself observes the law. During the periods of creation of this new earth, he set the example for us. It is recorded that:

"And on the seventh day God ended his work which he had made; and he rested on the seventh day from all his work which he had made.

"And God blessed the seventh day, and sanctified it: because that in it he had rested from all his work which God created and made." (Genesis 2:2-3.)

Since that day of rest, the Lord has continued to urge us to follow his example. I believe we can all recall Moses and his people in the wilderness as they ate the manna provided each day for them. But some of the Israelites were surprised on the Sabbath when they found none. They had been warned by Moses in these words: "Six days ye shall gather it; but on the seventh day, which is the sabbath, in it there shall be none" (Exodus 16:26).

Unfortunately, it takes some of us a long time to learn. And the Israelites had plenty of time to do so. They ate manna for forty years. Imagine! The next time you are tempted to complain about eating your broccoli, consider that possibility and be grateful.

Earlier I mentioned that there are those who would like us to believe that keeping the Sabbath day holy really doesn't work; that it doesn't pay; that it doesn't "fill up your reserve tank." If they could, they would vote out the Sabbath. In fact, many have tried. Let me share with you a clever statement on how they attempt to do so.

"Last Sunday I voted to close the church—not intentionally, nor maliciously—but carelessly, thoughtlessly, lazily, indifferently, I voted. I voted to close its doors that its witness and its testimony might be stopped.

"I voted to close the open Bible—the Bible that had been given us by years of struggle and by the blood of martyrs who died that we might have it to read. I voted to stop preaching the glorious truths of the gospel. I voted that the children of the Sunday School no longer be taught the stories of the Bible and no longer lift their voices in singing.

"I voted for the voice of the choir and the congregation to be stilled, and that they no longer sing in united praise. I voted for every missionary of the Church to be called home, every local worker to stop preaching, every hospital, every school, to close. I voted every missionary project be abandoned, every influence for good, for right and truth in our community to be curtailed and finally stopped.

"I voted for the darkness of superstition, the degrading influence of sin, the blight of ignorance, and the curse of selfish greed once again to settle their damning load on the shoulders of an already overburdened world.

"I voted for all this. For you see, I could have gone and I should have gone, but I didn't. I stayed away from church last Sunday." (Albert L. Zobell, *Story Sermons* [Bookcraft Publishers, 1954], p. 36.)

It would be interesting for each of us to take a quiz on how well we filled up our reserve tanks last Sunday. Then, for those who failed, it would be fun to give an essay test on why they didn't take advantage of the Sabbath. Two ministers did something like that. They made up a list of timeworn excuses people use for not going to church, which is part of keeping the Sabbath day holy. Then they applied these excuses to something most people enjoy doing—going to a movie. I think you will enjoy this short list. If nothing else, it makes a point that is hard to dispute and one worth considering.

"I don't attend the movies anymore because the manager of the theater has never visited me.

"I did go a few times, but no one spoke to me. Those who go there are not very friendly.

"Every time I go they ask for money.

"Not all folks who go to the movies live up to the high standards of the film.

"I went to the movies so much as a child I have decided I have had all the entertainment I need.

"The performance lasts too long. I can't sit still for an hour and a half.

"I don't always agree with what I hear and see there.

"I don't think they have very good music.

"The shows are held in the evening and that is the only time I have to be home with my family."

Not bad reasoning!

From a seminary teacher's outline here is the story of a young man who understood the blessing of the Sabbath and the earthly and spiritual reward of keeping it holy:

"Johnny Mitchell, the son of a Filipino father and a Chinese-Hawaiian mother, lived with his family in the tiny dock town of Mahukona in the district of Kohala on the Big Island of Hawaii. With his twin brothers, Fonso and Joseph, he played on the Kohala High School basketball team. He also served as the branch president with these twin brothers as his counselors.

"Johnny was selected to play on the all-star team, representing the Big Island. This would have brought honor to him, to his family, and to his community, but much to the surprise of everyone, Johnny turned down the honor. When questioned as to why he had made such a decision, he simply answered, 'Some of the games would have been played on the Sabbath.'

"Some of the officials could not understand why such an outstanding youth would spurn such an offer. Johnny had been taught to keep the Sabbath day holy, so he answered, 'When games and amusements are over, the Sabbath will still go on. *There will always be a Sabbath.*'

"Johnny was killed while fighting in Korea and lies buried in Punch Bowl Crater National Cemetery on the Island of Oahu, but his great conviction to keep the

Sabbath day holy will be remembered by all those who knew him." (Old Testament Teacher Manual, 1967.)

There will, in fact, always be a Sabbath. And it exists today for you and me. When we keep it holy and honor the Lord's day we can be assured that the Lord will . bless and strengthen and prosper our efforts during the rest of the week. Our reserve tanks will be filled to overflowing.

I submit that the station is open every Sunday and the process of filling the tank is simple. May I give the following Sabbath suggestions:

Rest—from daily labors.

Think—about the purpose of life and how we are *really* doing.

Show—gratitude through prayer and our Sabbath example.

Learn—spiritual truths by attending church and study of the scriptures.

Serve—others (including our own families) through church duties and acts of kindness.

This list is hardly all-inclusive, but it will give us a place to start.

Let me challenge each one to give it a try. If you already honor the Lord's day, do even better. If you do not now keep the Sabbath, try to do so. I bear witness that you will like how you feel not only on Sunday, but all week long. You will receive added strength and help during "your days" if you keep holy "his day."

May we be wise enough to take the counsel of the Lord and refill our tanks on Sunday. May we replenish our souls by our Sabbath actions. I remind you that the Sabbath is a holy day, not a holiday. And I bear witness from personal experience, that only those who live this law can know of its power and influence.

His Way

As I travel in my car, I often listen to the radio. I try to turn the dial enough so that I get a smattering of many stations. That way I hear a little news, some sports, some commentary and, of course, music. May I confess that there is one modern song I really struggle with (it is one of those rare ones I can understand). It is called "My Way" and extols the virtue of each man and woman doing their "own thing" in their own way. The final line, sung at approximately twenty-five thousand decibels, repeats the glorious declaration that the poor fellow did, in fact, do it his way. The exact line is, "I did it my way."

I have wanted to rewrite the lyrics to that song many times. I think the music has possibilities. I think the words are—well—shall we say, "representative" of a certain philosophy in our world today.

Now, if I could rewrite it, I would call it "His Way." Then, just as in the original, I would cite all the difficulties of life encountered by the vocalist and the last

line, still at twenty-five thousand decibels, would proclaim, "I did it *his* way." There is something to be said
for obedience in doing it *his* way!

Even as I share these feelings I hear the words of
the Savior in Gethsemane. He hesitated before drinking of the bitter cup. He asked that he might not have
to bleed from every pore. But when he came right up
against it, he uttered some of the most profound words
ever spoken: "Nevertheless not my will, but thine, be
done" (Luke 22:42).

I don't know about you, but those words do not
always come easily to my lips. Sometimes we want
what we want, and at whatever cost. A friend of mine
prayed over a personal matter for several weeks.
Finally, the answer came. It was an impression which
said to my friend, "No!" And being mortal, he knelt
again and said, "Heavenly Father, perhaps you didn't
understand what I said..." Oh, how difficult it is
sometimes to do it *his* way.

And how difficult it is sometimes to teach that
great principle to others. Especially teenagers! Here is
a story of a father who tried. And, amazingly, he did a
pretty good job of it:

"Jesse and his father were making a long
automobile trip. Along the way they had been
discussing the son's behavior at home and how he had
done several things he had been told not to do. This
discussion led to a sermon by his father about the
importance of commandments, rules, laws and advice.
Jesse angrily told his father that he was seventeen
now, old enough to know what was right and what was
wrong, and he didn't need anybody or any rules to tell
him what to do. Feeling that any more discussion
would just cause the argument to get worse, Jesse's
father said nothing more.

"They were soon approaching a fork in the road.
There were two signs marking the way. One pointed to

their destination, the other to a direction away from where they were going. When they reached the fork, the father suddenly turned the steering wheel towards the wrong road. Jesse shouted, 'Dad, you're going the wrong way. The sign says the other way.' He pushed the gas pedal to the floor and the car zoomed down along the wrong road. Then the father said firmly, 'I don't care what the sign said, I'm old enough to make up my own mind. No road sign is going to tell *me* which direction to go.'

"As his father slowed the car down and prepared to turn around, he looked at Jesse. He was blushing. There was no need to say more." (Adapted from a story by Sterling W. Sill.)

It takes a smart father to think that fast. In fact, it takes a good father and mother to attempt to teach such a principle in the first place. But it really does need to be taught.

Some other mothers and fathers I know were also successful in teaching their sons. Their story is scripture, but is not as well known as some. It concerns a group of young fighting men who were brought to battle against an almost overwhelming army of the enemy. However, the Lord blessed them and they were victorious. In fact, they were so successful that not one of these fine young men was killed. Now, I've fought in some intense battles in World War II, but I have never seen an army unit without one fatality. The scriptures explain why these young men were saved:

"Yea, and they did obey and observe to perform every word of command with exactness; yea, and even according to their faith it was done unto them; and I did remember the words which they said unto me that their mothers had taught them" (Alma 57:21).

Did you notice that word? Exactness! They obeyed with exactness. What a compliment! And then, of course, you heard who got the credit for their faith:

their mothers. And it was well deserved, as most faithful young men can testify.

Things haven't really changed much. One year while I was watching the New Year's Day bowl games on TV (between roast beef, snacks and grandkids), a couple of things became very clear to me. Certainly the most obvious were the penalties and the part they played in the victories (or losses). When the rules were broken, the team paid. There were some exciting drives nullified by penalties. And there were some touchdowns scored because the defense was caught "disobeying the rules." Some young men just had to try it "their way."

But the thing that sent a chill or two up my spine that day was to watch the winners as the gun sounded. There were tears, hugging, back-slapping, "high-fives" and coaches on shoulders. And in general, just plain old happiness. I imagine that winning by the rules will always be a lot more fun than losing. That's the way it is when you obey.

Abraham Lincoln put it better than I: "When I do good, I feel good. When I don't do good, I don't feel good."

That's about as plain as it can be. And that is the whole reason for doing things *his* way. When we obey him and live his commandments, we are happy. When we don't we are not.

This is the way to judge whether we are doing what we should. Will what we want to do make us happy—I mean really happy? Will it make our parents, spouse or children happy? And when I say happy, I don't mean temporary satisfaction or fun. I mean real happiness, even joy which lasts forever. Or will what we want to do bring unhappiness to us and to our families. Not merely temporary disappointment but deep sorrow which would affect our families or our whole lives.

May I give you my assurance that obedience really does bring happiness. God does live! He does care! And he has given us laws that, if we observe them, will bring happiness now and eternal life in his presence in the future. That is what it is all about.

May we learn and study his commandments and then may we do them with exactness.

The Grass
Is Greener

I am not Swedish, but there is an old Swedish folktale which I like. It has a profound meaning for us in our day, especially with all the affluence about us.

It seems there was a very poor couple who eked out an existence on their farm. One winter evening three strangers came to their door and asked for shelter for the night. This good couple had little of this world's goods but gave the visitors all that they could. In the morning the three men were gone, but from that instant the farmer and his wife began to prosper. In a short time they were rich.

Their neighbors, who were already wealthy, began to covet the new-found prosperity of the couple. But their turn came, for one evening the three men knocked on the door of the envious neighbors. They were delighted. They treated their guests with every courtesy. The following morning, as the strangers left, they told the couple that their next three wishes would be granted.

You can imagine their excitement. In fact, I can imagine how I would feel. I am not sure what my three wishes would be, but one would involve golf clubs and a lower handicap. And there is a great golf course I know of in Spain.

Anyway, our rich friends had their own troubles. They couldn't decide on the three wishes. Let me quote from the ending of the story:

"The farmer could not decide between more land or more cattle, or whether to wish for both. The wife was torn between the desire for a diamond necklace and the necessity of owning an ermine coat.

" 'Another fur coat!' stormed the farmer. 'I wish you had been born with fur so that you'd stop all this talk of fur coats, once and for all!'

"No sooner had he spoken than, to his horror, his wife turned into a large white weasel.

" 'You beast!' she screamed to her husband when she saw what she had become. 'How I wish you didn't have a tongue in your head!'

"And so it happened! The farmer was speechless. No more wishes for him!

"There was now but one wish left and only the wife could make it. 'Oh,' she sobbed, 'How I wish we had never wished for anything but had been happy with our own good fortune!'

"This turned out to be the best wish of all. The farmer regained his tongue, the wife lost her resemblance to a weasel, and for once they truly became content." (Retold by Ann Stacey, *Highlights*.)

The last four words are profound in their simplicity; "they truly became content." Not bad advice. I have found that in life the grass is not always greener on the other side of the fence. It may look to be, but when we cross over, we find the grass filled with weeds and rocks and rubbish. Then, from a new perspective, our own lawn looks amazingly plush. But all too often, there is no way to go back.

Through the Apostle Paul, the Lord gave us all some excellent advice. I repeat it now as encouragement to think seriously before we rip our jeans scrambling wildly over the fence. Paul said, "For I have learned, in whatsoever state I am, therewith to be content" (Philippians 4:11).

I find it reassuring that Paul uses the phrase "for I have learned." That is how most of us finally come to recognize our own good fortune. I remember hearing an old saying that if we all took our troubles and hung them on the line, we would probably go back and reclaim our own rather than risk trying someone else's. Being content with our current situation is a great virtue.

Now, I wouldn't want anyone to believe I think we shouldn't improve our lot in life. We should! We should always be seeking to improve ourselves, whether financially, educationally, physically, spiritually, or otherwise. But, in the process, we should be content with our life. Always looking ahead can rob us of the joy of right now. I have some good friends who were called to go to a foreign country to spend several years. But I will tell you a secret—they packed their bags, and when they got there, they *unpacked* them and settled in. They were content to stay there for as long as they were needed.

Looking over that fence continually can cause us grief. It can also cause us embarrassment. Things are not always as they seem. That fact was reinforced in my mind by a story on the importance of looking before leaping, and then not leaping at all:

"A New York executive boarded the subway one morning for the trip downtown to his office. No seats were available so he held onto one of the poles near the center.

"When the train made an express stop at 42nd Street a small, well-dressed man entered the doors, bumped into the executive, then turned and headed back toward the doors.

"Instinctively the businessman felt for his wallet which he kept in his inside coat pocket. It was gone! He leaped after the small man and, just as the doors were closing, reached out and grabbed the other by his coat collar.

"The doors slid together, their rubber edges closing on the man's arm, but he held on. The train started to move and suddenly the jacket tore free. The executive was left holding the man's ripped coat.

"During the rest of the trip downtown the executive grew more angry and despondent. What kind of city was it where a man could not go to work in the morning without having his pocket picked?

"He reached his office ready to quit his business, sell his home and move to the country. As he was preparing to call the police, his phone rang. It was his wife calling to tell him that he had left his wallet at home." (*Highlights*, January 1971.)

On another occasion, Paul again advised us to be happy with what we already have. He said: "Let your conversation be without covetousness; and be content with such things as ye have: for he hath said, I will never leave thee, nor forsake thee" (Hebrews 13:5).

I submit that being content with what we have, especially spiritually, is a great blessing. We should seek seriously and consistently for the truth. But when we find it, we should be happy with it and the peace it brings. Again, that doesn't mean that we should sit

still. We should and must progress. That is an eternal
principle. Progress is everlasting. But *in the process*
we should be happy to look at our own grass instead of
the neighbor's. It is a little bit like a clever statement I
read: "The difference between a cute little rascal and a
potential juvenile delinquent is whether he is your
child or somebody else's." I really believe that cute
rascal will always be found in our own yard, on our
own grass.

Let us learn to be content with our current station
in life, for it will bring great joy. In addition, many
ulcers and migraines will go away. Spiritually and
emotionally, enjoying what we have right now is great
therapy. It's what the Lord expects. So, no matter how
difficult it may seem, there are parents to be enjoyed,
children to be loved, friends to be cherished and
beauty to be seen. May we do so. May we understand
that in the process of eternal growth, being content
with what a loving Father in Heaven has given us is
not only a sign of maturity, but a means of being truly
happy in this life.

Hang in There

Sometimes it's difficult to see the end from the beginning. We get so wrapped up in the here and now and so bogged down with present cares that it's hard not to give up. I was so reminded by a short quote I read the other day:

"When nothing seems to help, I go and look at a stone-cutter hammering away at his rock, perhaps a hundred times without as much as a crack showing in it. Yet, at the hundred and first blow it will split in two, and I know it was not that blow that did it, but all that had gone before."

The author of that bit of wisdom, Jacob Riis, knew something we often lose sight of—continued blows will finally split a rock if we just hang in there. We can succeed in life if we just stick with it. Persistence is an eternal quality.

I find the story of an old gentleman's advice not only useful, but true:

"A reporter was interviewing an old gentleman on his hundredth birthday. 'To what do you attribute your longevity?'

"The old man thought for a moment, then replied, 'I never smoked, I never drank liquor, never fooled around with women, and always got up at six every morning.'

"The reporter duly noted the old man's formula, then commented, 'I had an uncle who did the same thing but he only lived to eighty. How do you account for that?'

"'Simple,' said the old man, 'he didn't keep at it long enough.'"

I am constantly inspired by the Apostle Paul's references to the need to endure and persist. He took his own advice and did, in fact, persist faithfully to the end. And in doing so, he offered hope to us. While in Rome for the second time, he wrote the following:

"For I am now ready to be offered, and the time of my departure is at hand.

"I have fought a good fight, I have finished my course, I have kept the faith:

"Henceforth there is laid up for me a crown of righteousness, which the Lord, the righteous judge, shall give me at that day: and not to me only, but unto all them also that love his appearing." (2 Timothy 4:6-8.)

Paul's assurance that a reward is available to all of us is predicated on the fact that we, too, must persist. We also must fight the good fight, finish our course, and keep the faith. It sounds pretty hard, but it surely beats the alternative. Paul kept the commandments of the Lord from the time the truth was first introduced to him. We can do the same.

May I suggest one simple help in our effort to persist—it's not the only help available, but it works. Let me refer again to a bit of advice I read:

"The American painter, John Sargent, once painted a panel of roses which was highly praised by critics. It was a small picture, but it approached perfection.

"Although offered a high price for it on many occasions, Sargent refused to sell it. He considered it his best work and was very proud of it.

"Whenever he was deeply discouraged and doubtful of his abilities as an artist, he would look at it and remind himself, 'I painted that.' Then his confidence and ability would come back to him.

"There are times when all of us doubt our ability. And the harder the work we do, the more creative it is, the more vulnerable we are to such doubts.

"We can't live on past achievements, but we can use them for inspiration as Sargent had the wisdom to do. Everyone should have a 'highwater mark' to look back to—something he can be proud of and say, 'I did that and it is good. And because I did it once, I can do it again.'"

When we get discouraged, persisting is much easier when we recall some of our past spiritual highlights. They help to reinforce the fact that we did it once and can do it again. It is very much as Babe Ruth said when asked what he thought about when he struck out. The Babe answered, "I think about hitting home runs."

Now, I am almost certain that some will say, "Well, I've never hit a home run," or religiously speaking, "I'm not sure I've ever had a spiritual reassurance or experience that I can fall back on." I submit that we all have. There is not one of us so bad that we haven't done much good and lived the great majority of the commandments. That being true, let us remember how we felt when we did so. I can recall my youth vividly, and I can remember the feelings I had when I was "a good boy." I am constantly urged to persist in doing better because of those feelings. We can all draw strength from our past if we take the time to do so.

Here's additional food for thought to help us in our efforts to righteously persist. I want to remind you of a great man.

"Many years ago a man emerged from an alcoholic nightmare in a small hospital on New York's Central Park West. A doctor was standing at his bedside. 'Morning, Bill.'

" 'Morning, Doc.'

" 'Would it interest you to know this is your fiftieth visit?'

"The emaciated, sick man in the bed smiled weakly. 'That calls for a celebration, Doc. How about a drink?'

"The doctor sighed.

" 'I'm a hopeless case, huh?'

" 'I'm afraid so. But I'll tell you what I'll do. You can have your drink if you'll first do something for me.'

" 'Anything—so long as I get my drink.'

" 'They brought in a young man last night—his first time. He's down the hall. I'd like to help him.'

" 'What can I do?'

" 'Just go see him. Let him take a good look at you. It might scare him enough to stop.'

"A few minutes later the old alcoholic stumbled into the young man's room. He didn't denouce drinking but he told the boy that there were simply some people who couldn't take it. A man should find out in time—before it ruined the rest of his life, as it had his.

"The younger man was sullen, but the other persisted. As he talked a strange thing began to happen. He said things, remembered things from the past, that surprised even him.

"He wanted more than anything in the world to stop this young man from going the route he had taken. Maybe it was the memory of his own wasted life—how he had disappointed his parents, his family. All he knew was that the more he talked, the more he had a mission in life—to stop this young man from drinking.

"'Only a power greater than yourself can stop you from becoming like me,' he told the boy.

"'I don't believe in God,' the young man snorted.

"'Maybe I don't either, but I know this: The bottle is stronger than you are. You can't do it by yourself, any more than I could. Will you let me help? Maybe we could help each other...'

"All morning they talked. At the end both swore never to take another drink, and if the urge was too strong, they would call each other for help.

"The older man stuck to his promise.

"He returned to hospitals after that, but not as a patient. He came to help other alcoholics in his role as co-founder of one of the world's most successful organizations, Alcoholics Anonymous." (*Bits and Pieces.*)

That's an amazing story and clearly suggests good counsel. When persisting, it's a great advantage to have the help of others who are trying also to persist. That not only makes sense, but it works. When we get discouraged, talking to someone who is also "fighting the good fight" will help.

The Apostle Peter was that kind of a man. He knew what it was like to persevere in difficult circumstances. We find it perfectly logical to see him out helping others. On one occasion, together with John, Peter went up to the temple in Jerusalem. He found at the gate of the temple a lame man begging alms. His request to Peter was not denied. As it is recorded by Luke:

"Then Peter said, Silver and gold have I none; but such as I have give I thee: In the name of Jesus Christ of Nazareth rise up and walk.

"And he took him by the right hand, and lifted him up: and immediately his feet and ankle bones received strength." (Acts 3:6-7.)

Isn't that a marvelous phrase, "And he took him by the right hand, and lifted him up." Sometimes, persisting would seem impossible without help from others.

In conclusion, there are two suggestions previously made on being persistent. First, let us continually recall our former successes. Second, let us help and be helped by others who are also in the struggle. Let me add to those two, several others I have found helpful:

1. Pray daily.
2. Read the scriptures regularly. (Regularly is not once a year.)
3. Repent of misdeeds.
4. Live the commandments the best you can.
5. Serve those around you.
6. When all else fails, simply hang on.

I am convinced that we can all do much better in our righteous persistence. We have been commanded to do so and if our Father asks us to do it, we can. He knows us. He knows our capacity. He knows our limitations. With all that, he has still asked that we do it.

May we think seriously on these things and do them. May we resolve to do those simple things that will help us persist and take us back to the presence of our Heavenly Father.

Courage Each Day

Having served in the Armed Forces during World War II, I can appreciate great acts of courage. I have seen many myself. Men do great and noble deeds when they are called upon to do so.

Such a man was Major Bernard Fisher, a pilot for the Air Force stationed in Vietnam. Major Fisher has a motto which guides his life. It is simple! He asks the question, "Is it right or is it wrong?" Not a bad question, even for civilians.

Major Fisher had an opportunity to ask that question many times. But one case in particular remains in my mind. Several hundred of our American fighting men were trapped in the Ashau Valley by the Vietcong and were being supported by Major Fisher and five other fighter planes. On one of their runs, a plane went down, but the pilot managed to get out and hide by the side of a deserted runway. He was surrounded by the enemy.

It was then Major Fisher had to decide whether or not to risk his life and try to rescue his companion. At the same time he asked himself the question, "Is it right or is it wrong?" Having made the decision, he landed at the air strip and managed to pull the pilot aboard and take off again. His plane was bullet-riddled and the tires of his jet were shredded to ribbons, but neither of the men had a scratch on him. It was an incredible feat of courage. The recommendation for Major Fisher to receive the Congressional Medal of Honor reads, in part:

"He performed this rescue in the face of some 2,000 armed and nearly victorious hostile troops. His determination, his incredible display of courage in the face of resolute and heavily armed hostile force, his complete disregard for his own life to effect the rescue of a fellow airman, and his resolve to continue despite advice by others of the severe hazards involved, reflect the highest ideals of American fighting forces above and beyond the call of duty. I personally hold no reservations in recommending Major Bernard F. Fisher for the Medal of Honor." (Lt. Gen. J. H. Moore, Commander, 7th Air Force, Vietnam.)

By the way, he received the medal.

Now, for a moment, let's shift to another time and place. The young man's name is Joseph. He has been sold into Egypt by his jealous brothers, but has managed to find favor in the eyes of his master, Potiphar. Potiphar's wife, however, has designs on Joseph and, at the appropriate (or inappropriate) time, propositions him.

Now, there is no one around who will know. It could be "their secret." Neither is there a battle raging on every side. No bombs are falling; no artillery shells are fired. There is only a fine young man trying to protect his great gift—his virtue! But, just as surely as Major Fisher felt the heat of battle and the threat to his life, so Joseph felt the battle within and the threat to his life—his eternal life.

Joseph, too, was victorious. And in his victory, instead of receiving a medal of honor, he spoke these deeply significant words: "How then can I do this great wickedness, and sin against God?" (Genesis 39:9.)

I submit that there are many kinds of courage. They are all important, and they all require doing— some are physical, some are moral, some are social, some are intellectual. But, may I also suggest that there is a kind of courage which may require all of these I just mentioned. It is a rather quiet courage and is required by each of us on a daily basis; that is, if we want to be happy and successful. It is of the intensity required of a Major Fisher or a Joseph, and it is demonstrated in our lives as we try to live "Just for today."

"Just for today I will be happy. This assumes that what Abraham Lincoln said is true, that 'Most folks are about as happy as they make up their minds to be.' Happiness is from within; it is not a matter of externals.

"Just for today I will try to adjust myself to what is and not try to adjust everything to my own desires. I will take my family, my business, and my luck as they come and fit myself to them.

"Just for today I will take care of my body. I will exercise it, care for it, nourish it, and not abuse it or neglect it so that it will be a perfect machine for my bidding.

"Just for today I will try to strengthen my mind. I will learn something useful. I will not be a mental loafer. I will read something that requires effort, thought, and concentration.

"Just for today I will exercise my soul in these ways: I will do somebody a good turn and not get found out. I will do at least two things I don't want to do, as William James suggests, just for exercise.

"Just for today I will be agreeable. I will look as well as I can, dress as becomingly as possible, talk low, act courteously, be liberal with praise, criticize not at all, nor find fault with anything, and not try to regulate nor improve anyone.

"Just for today I will try to live through this day only, not tackle my whole life problem at once. I can do things for twelve hours that would appall me if I had to keep them up for a lifetime.

"Just for today I will have a program. I will write down what I expect to do every hour. I may not follow it exactly, but I will have it. It will eliminate two pests, hurry and indecision.

"Just for today I will have a quiet half hour all by myself and relax. In this half hour sometimes I will think of God, so as to get a little more perspective to my life.

"Just for today I will be unafraid, especially I will not be afraid to be happy, to enjoy what is beautiful, to love, and to believe that those I love, love me." (Sibyl F. Partridge.)

That's what I call real courage! The courage to live one day at a time and to try to do it with dignity. I have seen people who couldn't do it. But for each one who couldn't, there are many, many who do.

We may rightfully ask ourselves how we are doing. And while we are doing that we can also remind ourselves of the following quote from a very wise man: "Anytime the going seems easy, better check and see if you're going downhill."

It seems to me that we don't need to worry too much about that problem. With the challenges of the economy, jobs, permissiveness, and so forth, we have plenty to keep us going uphill. In fact, if life gets easy, we may want to enjoy it for a moment or two. It won't last! But one thing that will last is how we deal with our problems. I am reminded of the poem by Rudyard Kipling:

If you can keep your head when all about you
    Are losing theirs and blaming it on you,
If you can trust yourself when all men doubt you,
    But make allowance for their doubting too;
If you can wait and not be tired by waiting,
    Or being lied about, don't deal in lies,
Or being hated, don't give way to hating,
    And yet don't look too good, nor talk too wise:

If you can dream—and not make dreams your
    master;
    If you can think—and not make thoughts your
    aim;
If you can meet with Triumph and Disaster
    And treat those two impostors just the same;
If you can bear to hear the truth you've spoken
    Twisted by knaves to make a trap for fools,
Or watch the things you gave your life to, broken,
    And stoop and build 'em up with worn-out
    tools:

If you can make one heap of all your winnings
    And risk it on one turn of pitch-and-toss,
And lose, and start again at your beginnings
    And never breathe a word about your loss;
If you can force your heart and nerve and sinew
    To serve your turn long after they are gone,
And so hold on when there is nothing in you
    Except the Will which says to them: "Hold on!"

If you can talk with crowds and keep your virtue,
    Or walk with Kings—nor lose the common
    touch,

If neither foes nor loving friends can hurt you,
  If all men count with you, but none too much;
If you can fill the unforgiving minute
  With sixty seconds' worth of distance run,
Yours is the Earth and everything that's in it,
  And—which is more—you'll be a Man, my son!
                    (Rudyard Kipling, "If—".)

Now, let us not forget that a practical courage on a daily basis is what it's all about. We need courage to—
  face the dishes in the morning,
  clean and pick up after kids who know better,
  pay a bill partially instead of in full,
  get along with old clothes instead of new,
  drive a clunker instead of a Seville,
  be nice when there seems so little reason.
You name it, it takes courage.

I want you to know that life is good. The Lord intended that we be tried, but he also gave us the innate ability to handle life. Part of that ability is a deep-down courage to face it as it is. Major Fisher did it, as did Joseph. Millions have done it, including you and me. May we continue to do so, realizing that there is a power available from above. We can call on him if we will, and he will give us that extra strength for the day. Of this I am absolutely sure.

Hands

Amidst autumn's crisp beautifully colored days comes one of our most celebrated holidays, Thanksgiving. I imagine that in many homes families commemorate this special event in our history in some of the typical ways with family gatherings, turkey and dressing, pumpkin pie and Alka Seltzer. Somehow we correlate food and gratitude—the more we eat, the more thankful we are. I suppose if we follow that logic, teenagers are the most grateful of all.

Of course, not everyone has the luxury of a big Thanksgiving dinner and all that goes with it. Some have little, if any, food. But, somehow, most find something to be thankful for. Children are especially good at that. As I reflected about the ability of kids to find good in almost anything, I remembered a great little story that really proves the point. I don't know who the author is, but whoever it was knew what he was talking about. Let me share it with you in his own words:

"It was nearing Thanksgiving and the teacher had just given the children instructions to draw something for which they were very thankful.

"As she looked at the children she thought in her heart: These poor little children have so very little to be thankful for—half fed, half clothed—what would they draw that they were especially thankful for?

"Take David for instance. He was so thin and uncared-for, and so very shy. He didn't enter into the games with the other boys for he wasn't able to hold his own with them. Always when she was on duty on the playground, David would follow her about like a shadow and press very close to her as though for protection. What could he draw for which he was especially thankful?

"The drawings were completed and she held them up for the class to see. There were the usual turkeys, tables laden with good foods, etc., about which these poor children could only know from pictures.

"David had drawn a hand and when she held it up she got many responses from the children. One child said, 'That is the hand of God, for he gives us everything.' Another said, 'That represents all of the hands that help us.' But David had drawn only one. This drawing caused more comment than any of the others, but David offered no explanation.

"The teacher was curious, so when the others were busy working on their next assignment she leaned close to David and said, 'Whose hand are you especially grateful for, David?'

"Looking up into her face he simply said, 'Yours.'

"Then she remembered the numerous occasions when he had pressed closely to her and she had reached down and taken his hand in hers and pressed it warmly. She had given something of herself to this little boy that was most priceless to him and for which he was exceedingly grateful."

Hands! Of all the things we have to be grateful for, I wonder if one of the most important could be hands—a mother's or father's, a sister's or brother's, perhaps a friend's, or even a stranger's. In our modern world hands are often viewed as being destructive—hands of war, hands of crime, hands of violence and protest, hands of destruction. But I have more faith in the human race than that. From my own observation and experience I know that there are millions of helping hands—hands of kindness, hands of service, hands of consolation, hands of affection.

May I remind you that the counsel of a loving Heavenly Father has always been to lend a helping hand. It was he who said "succor the weak, lift up the hands which hang down, and strengthen the feeble knees" (D&C 81:5).

Now, isn't that a beautiful way of putting it? What a great way to put our hands to use—in succoring the poor, in lifting the hands of those who are literally and symbolically weak, and in strengthening the feeble.

The prophet Isaiah said it a little differently: "Strengthen ye the weak hands, and confirm the feeble knees. Say to them that are of a fearful heart, Be strong, fear not." (Isaiah 35:3-4.)

Can you picture that? Using our hand to put around the shoulder of a family member or friend (or even a stranger) and saying, "Now, don't be afraid. I'm here, and the Lord loves you. You'll be all right." I repeat, to do so is a commandment. Through Paul came the Lord's counsel: "Bear ye one another's burdens, and so fulfil the law of Christ" (Galatians 6:2).

So, once again, I wonder if perhaps we should be particularly grateful to those who have helped us along the way. Has there been any one of us who hasn't had a hand given to us in a moment of need? Has any one of us been so self-sufficient that we have progressed to our particular point in life without having had a pat on the back or an arm around our shoulder? I know there are those who say they have "made it on their own," but I really doubt that. That is like the man who bellowed, "I'm an atheist, thank God!" Simply denying something doesn't make it so. We have *all* had a hand extended to us sometime in life, even if only briefly. What a blessing that is!

Now, as I talk about hands, may I mention the most important hands in our lives—hands that we should love and accept with the greatest of all gratitude. They are not hands of wives or husbands, mothers or fathers, children or friends. These hands have scars in them. They were pierced by nails. They were resurrected. They will return to govern this earth. Above all, they can lift us by his atonement to eternal life—that is, if we accept him. It was Isaiah who testified that "his hand is stretched out still" (Isaiah 9:12).

That means now—today—for every one of us! Isn't that something to be grateful for? The Savior is willing to take us as we are and make us into the kind of men and women we need to be. His hands can mold us and make us fit to live with him. For that I will be eternally grateful! All we have to do is have faith in him, constantly and completely repent of our sins and receive his ordinances. In other words, we just need to live the gospel all our lives. And when you think of it, that isn't too bad a price. I am thankful.

Now, may I add my witness that hands are great. We ought to be thankful. And most importantly, we ought to show our gratitude by using our own hands to bless others. There are any number of things a hand can do:

hold other hands,
pat a back,

give a gentle caress,
rest on a shoulder,
tousle hair,
pray.

May I bear my witness that hands were given to us to use; to help and lift. I know the Savior did so for us. I also know we can find real happiness by doing the same for others. I pray that we may be truly grateful for those hands around us who help. May we show our gratitude by doing the same.

Time Out

I love sports and what they can teach us. The other night while I was watching a basketball game I heard the captain yell that familiar phrase, "time-out." The team ran to the sidelines to receive some instructions from the man who can give them some help—the coach. And he did.

Now, isn't it interesting that, generally speaking, a team calls time-out when they're in trouble—when they need to regroup? I can recall many times in my own baseball career when we'd call "time," and the catcher, or pitching coach, or manager would come to the mound and give me some instructions or encouragement. Somtimes the language was most colorful, but it almost always helped.

Well, what's that got to do with you and me? Life's something like the big game, you know, and there are times when we need a time-out. Have we loaded the bases while we continue to pitch high and wide? Are we fourth and one on the goal line with ten seconds left? Has our twenty point lead evaporated to two? Is our marriage in trouble? Is that personal weakness still not under control? Are the finances ready to pull us under? Is our family solidarity sitting on shifting sand? And, most important of all, are we trying to go it alone? Or have we been smart enough to call "time-out" to ask the coach for help?

I'm reminded of something I read just the other day. It seems a small boy tried to lift a heavy stone, but couldn't budge it. His father, watching, finally said, "Are you sure you're using *all* your strength?"

"Yes, I am!" the boy cried.

"No, you're not," said the father. "You haven't asked me to help you."

Well, let me just tell you that however tight the game seems right now, I know the coach and I know that he can help. There *is* a personal and loving God who knows all the plays. He understands the game. He understands you. And he understands what you need now to help you in your life. Talking to him is an easy thing, really. All you have to do is call, "Time-out. I've had it. I need help. I can't take any more of this running without seeing clearly where the bases are."

The Lord is not removed a thousand galaxies away from you. Would the coach leave his team to wander to another grandstand? No! He's there, just waiting for you to admit to yourself and to him how much you need his help. He'll help you with the crucial plays. Give you more muscle and heart when it looks like you're about to be beat. Whisper words of comfort when you are.

Every day has its moments when you need him. You feel fatigued and ready to scream at your children. Say a silent prayer first and let those angry words get caught in your throat. You just stopped for gasoline and can't believe the price. Your head aches; you're under pressure; nothing goes right. Stop where you are and take a time-out with the coach. His advice is never questionable and he'll never get sacked for having a losing team. He can help you to be a winner.

A tearful mother with a baby in her arms and three preschoolers admitted to her friends that she wouldn't have been able to get her little family organized and dressed that morning if she hadn't stopped in the middle of the chaos and said a little prayer. When she did, strength and patience flowed into her beyond her own reserves. The task that had seemed impossible only minutes before was easily done.

That is the nature of the Lord's help to us. Sometimes he will not change the task or the obstacle, but he will change us. Pure intelligence can flow into us from a source we hardly know. Oil can be poured on the troubled waters of our heart.

Florence Hansen was selected to sculpt a wonderful monument to women to be placed in a city garden in Nauvoo, Illinois. She is a gifted sculptor with a highly trained ability in her field and this chance for her was a chance of a lifetime, the kind of opportunity that only comes along rarely for an artist. She was given a month to come up with her conception for the monument to women, and every day she tried. She worked on it by the hour. The thoughts teased at her mind. But the more hours she spent at her task, the more frustrated she became. A monument to all women—past, present and future; a monument to the heroic, the grand, and invisible. The task seemed almost overwhelming to her, and her efforts seemed not to match up to her lofty assignment. She had the mechanical ability for the task. She knew that, but something was missing. After a month of trying, after all the vain hours staring at lumps of clay that remained only that—lumps—she felt that perhaps she had failed. Maybe she wasn't the one to sculpt this wonderful monument to women.

Finally, at the end of those thirty long days, the one who had commissioned her for the task called to see how she was coming along. She had to admit that she had done nothing on it *yet*, but could she just have one more day?

The next day went much the same as had the past thirty. She sketched out many ideas, but none seemed grand enough. She had clearly failed. At quarter after three she went to the phone to call and report that she was not the one to do the monument, but just as she had dialed part of the number she stopped, thinking she should give it just forty-five more minutes.

She had prayed many times about the assignment before her, sculpting a lovely monument to be placed in a city, but she took time to pray again, and this time something special happened. Pure intelligence seemed to flow into her. She got up from her knees and went to the shapeless clay. Her fingers and thoughts seemed to move without effort. Her mind was clear of self-doubt and the conception for the monument came easily. In forty-five minutes she knew what the statue should look like. She accomplished in forty-five minutes what she had not been able to do in thirty days, because this time she had help. She was inspired. And her lovely statue to women everywhere stands today completed in a garden in Nauvoo.

Well, the Lord does answer prayers like that. He gives us insight; he gives us strength for the tasks ahead; he gives us direction for our lives. We just need to take time out to call on him. Wouldn't it be sad to ignore him and then when you've finished playing the game find out you've been in the wrong ball park the whole time? Or as someone else put it, be like those who "climb the ladder of success only to find the ladder has been leaning on the wrong wall."

I suppose the question is, Are we willing to ask the coach? Are we willing to pay the simple price of kneeling down and finding out for ourselves that he lives and what he wants us to do? And again, are we willing to *do* what he counsels? There's many an athlete who has found himself with an "early retirement" because he wouldn't follow instructions. He knew more than the coach. As I remember it, I tried never to be like that. But there are plenty who are. Just knowing a coach won't do, but knowing and listening and doing surely will.

When the game gets tight and we are harried, let's call "time-out" and seek our coach, our Eternal Father. Let's ask him where we stand. How can we tighten our defense? Are there some glaring weaknesses that the enemy is trying to exploit? How can we be a better husband, wife, mother, father, son or daughter, brother or sister? The coach knows and he will tell us.

I promise you if you'll humble yourself before a kind Heavenly Father, he'll find you help. Thank him. Ask. Listen. Ponder. Little by little, day by day you'll come to know him and recognize his counsel. He'll make this the best year of your life. It won't all be easy, but it will be bearable. And life will become increasingly happy despite the challenge.

May I bear you my witness that the reward for seeking him and finding him will be a much more peaceful life now and eternal joy with your loved ones in his presence. He's the most wise and glorious counselor of all. I know him. I love him. And I challenge us all to seek him diligently.

Producing Pearls

I have a friend who lived in a large city on the East Coast of the United States. He was a senior at a fine university and active on the debate team. He was also a religious young man who enjoyed studying the scriptures.

One day while reading them at the university library, a friend of his asked him what he was doing. My friend took the opportunity to explain to him as best he could how important he thought it was to learn more about the Lord and his church. His friend's reply went something like this: "Well, I guess it's all right to spend that kind of time if you really believe in God. Personally, I have a hard time believing in a God when there is so much hate in the world. If there is a God, why does he allow the wars and murders, the terror and suffering that are so prevalent in the world?"

If you were put in that position, what would you have said? How would you have answered?

Here is another good question: If God really exists, which he does, couldn't he prevent all of the horror and suffering that takes place? The answer is an obvious *yes!* He could! They why doesn't he?

A prophet has helped to answer that difficult question. Note carefully his answer:

"If all the sick for whom we pray were healed, if all the righteous were protected and the wicked destroyed, the whole program of the Father would be annulled and the basic principle of the gospel, free agency, would be ended. No man would live by faith.

"If joy and peace and rewards were instantaneously given the doer of good, there could be no evil — all would do good but not because of the rightness of doing good. There would be no test of strength, no development of character, no growth of powers, no free agency, only satanic controls." (Spencer W. Kimball, *Tragedy or Destiny?* Deseret Book Co., 1977, p. 3.)

As long as man has his agency, we will go right on having problems. Through them we grow and develop and progress. It is one of the divine purposes of mortality. We see it all around us. That very theme was the inspiration to a favorite piece of poetry:

> There once was an oyster, whose story I tell,
> Who found that some sand got under his shell
> Just one little grain, but it gave him a pain
> For oysters have feeling for all they're so plain.
> Now did he berate the workings of fate
> Which had led him to such a deplorable state?
> Did he curse the government or cry for an election?
> And cry that the seas should give him protection.
> No! He said to himself as he lay on the shelf,
> "Since I cannot remove it, I'll try to improve it."
> The years rolled around as the years always do.
> And he came to his ultimate destiny, stew.
> And the small grain of sand that bothered him so

Was a beautiful pearl all richly aglow.
The tale has a moral, for isn't it grand
What an oyster can do with a morsel of sand.
What couldn't we do, if we'd only begin
With all the things that get under our skin!
("The Oyster." Authorship unknown.)

What a marvelous principle! I submit that grains of adversity, although uncomfortable, can refine us right into perfection—not all at once, but day by day, year by year—even if it takes into eternity. Christ himself knew the price. Even though Jesus was perfect, Paul tells us one of the keys:

"Though he were a Son, yet learned he obedience by the things which he suffered;

"And being made perfect, he became the author of eternal salvation unto all them that obey him." (Hebrews 5:8-9.)

If you and I can just be obedient through all our trials and tribulations, the sand in our shells will have been worth it. We'll produce pearls instead of bee-bees; we'll act like oysters instead of crabs. It's all up to us!

Now, in the process of enduring our adversities, we might as well do our best to be pleasant. I admit it isn't easy. I know from experience, as you all do. But as some wise soul said: "If life gives you lemons, make lemonade."

Thomas Paine once put it: "I love the man who can smile in trouble, who can gather strength in distress and grow brave by reaction. 'Tis the business of little minds to shrink, but he whose heart is firm and whose conscience approves his conduct, will pursue his principles to the death."

May I suggest that, indeed, we can pursue our principles to the end. We can endure our trials, and we can be loved because we do it with a smile. I like the attitude of Thomas Paine and I like the attitude of a man described in an article I read:

"During a flood in California, a TV writer whose home was washed away discovered he had musical talent. 'My wife held onto a bed and floated down the canyon,' he said to a friend. 'How does that prove you have musical ability?' 'I accompanied her on the piano.'"

I'll admit that that's kind of corny. But I'll also be the one to praise the man for finding something to smile about in an otherwise "un-smile-able" situation. If we could just learn, or should I say *train* ourselves, we could endure more than we think we can.

Finally, let me put a proper perspective on the subject of adversity. After all is said and done, there is really only one power that can bring us through our personal difficulties. It is our Heavenly Father. He lives! He can do it! If he takes a hand in our lives, so can we. Let me give you a small verse of eight lines that says it all:

> I do not ask to walk smooth paths
> Nor bear an easy load.
> I pray for strength and fortitude
> To climb the rock-strewn road.
>
> Give me such courage I can scale
> The hardest peaks alone
> And transform every stumbling block
> Into a stepping stone.
>
> (Gail Brook Burket.)

As surely as we live, there is power available to us in our time of great need. His power can bless and sustain when nothing else can. As Job said after all had been taken from him: "For I know that my redeemer liveth" (Job 19:25). That is also my witness.

Truly, every stumbling block can become a stepping stone. Adversity can become our salvation, not our destruction. Our Father can lift us if we will call on him with faith. And if we will rise from our knees and use our agency to do *his* will and keep his commandments the best we can, he will sustain us.

I Know
This Man

Those of you who have either seen the movie *Ben Hur* or read the book have enjoyed one of the finest stories of our generation. It is a classic. I am willing to admit that I have seen it several times. The last time I watched, I was impressed with a line that I had never noticed before. It is a powerful statement and bears repeating.

You will remember Ben Hur as he is led prisoner en route to the galley of a Roman ship; tired, burned by the sun, thirsty beyond measure and denied water by the Roman guard, he is given water by a simple carpenter. That scene of compassion by the Lord, while he majestically "stares down" the Roman centurion, is one of the great scenes of the film. As I watched that incident, I thought upon these words by Shakespeare:

His life was gentle, and the elements
So mix'd in him, that Nature might stand up,
And say to all the world, this was a man.
                    (William Shakespeare, *Julius Caesar*.)

Indeed he was: the Son of God!

Then recall with me that moment late in the story when Ben Hur, with his mother and sister, searches for Jesus, only to find him being led, struggling with his cross, to Calvary. This time Ben Hur gives water to the Lord and, as he looks into his eyes, realizes he has seen the Master before. It is then that Ben Hur utters the powerful line I referred to earlier—that great statement of recognition: "I know this man!"

Now, without being presumptuous, and with an understanding of what that statement implies, I wish to add my witness that I, too, know this man. And just as surely as I know him, I know that we all can come to that knowledge. After all, it was Jesus himself who said: "And this is life eternal, that they might know thee the only true God, and Jesus Christ, whom thou hast sent" (John 17:3). And if it is a commandment, a wise Father in Heaven will help us find the way to keep it.

As I bear my testimony of Christ, let me share some feelings I have about him. Above all else, he loves us. I have felt his love in my life, personally, and have seen his tender concern for us all. We may doubt it, but it is there nevertheless. I share with you another testimony written by an author unknown to me:

"One night a man had a dream. He dreamed he was walking along the beach with the Lord. Across the sky flashed scenes from his life. For each scene, he noticed two sets of footprints in the sand: one belonging to him, and the other to the Lord.

"When the last scene flashed before him, he looked back at the footprints and noticed that many times along the path there was only one set of footprints in the sand. He also noticed that this happened during the lowest and saddest times in his life.

"This really bothered him, so he questioned the Lord. 'Lord, you said that once I decided to follow you,

you would walk with me all the way, but I noticed that during the most troublesome times of my life, there was only one set of footprints. I don't understand why, when I needed you the most, you deserted me.'

"The Lord replied, 'My precious, precious child, I love you and would never leave you. During your times of trial and suffering, when you see only one set of footprints, it was then that I carried you.'"

I share with you my witness that on occasion he has also carried me. In my darkest hours I have had a wonderful awareness that he has sustained me. He has lifted us all, even though we may hesitate to recognize him.

May I also declare with certainty that Jesus Christ is an actual being—that he lives. Even his early apostles doubted the reality and literalness of his resurrection. But, doubts notwithstanding, it was and is a fact.

"And as they thus spake, Jesus himself stood in the midst of them, and saith unto them, Peace be unto you.

"But they were terrified and affrighted, and supposed that they had seen a spirit.

"And he said unto them, Why are ye troubled? and why do thoughts arise in your hearts?

"Behold my hands and feet, that it is I myself: handle me, and see; for a spirit hath not flesh and bones, as ye see me have.

"And when he had thus spoken, he shewed them his hands and his feet.

"And while they yet believed not for joy, and wondered, he said unto them, Have ye here any meat?

"And they gave him a piece of broiled fish, and of an honeycomb.

"And he took it, and did eat before them. . . .

"Then opened he their understanding, that they might understand the scriptures,

"And said unto them, Thus it is written, and thus it behoved Christ to suffer, and to rise from the dead the third day:

"And that repentance and remission of sins should be preached in his name among all nations, beginning at Jerusalem.

"And ye are witnesses of these things." (Luke 24:36-43, 45-48.)

I too am his witness, and do so knowing that he is as real as we are. He exists. He lives. He is our elder brother. His is now a perfected and glorified body of flesh and bones. Such was his own testimony and in such a state we can also stand before him if we will.

May I also suggest that he had a divine purpose to his life which is unavoidably connected to ours. I quote his own words: "For behold, this is my work and my glory—to bring to pass the immortality and eternal life of man" (Moses 1:39).

It is both his work and his glory to reach out and save us. That was the reason for his life, and the giving of it. I also know that we must reach up to him. Sometimes that seems hard. Carlene Petree puts her testimony of the Savior into poetry:

> I am the rock.
> So stubborn,
> So resistant
> To change.
>
> And He
> Is the water.
> Gently
> And subtly
> Changing me
> Day by day.
>
> (Carlene Petree, "Resistance,"
> *Ensign,* December 1977, p. 59.)

The change does take place. But it happens one day at a time. There is no instant salvation. And once we are willing to acknowledge that fact, and do his will instead of ours, he can work miracles with us. The first step is our own attitude.

> "Father, where shall I work today?"
>   And my love flowed warm and free.
> Then he pointed me out a tiny spot
>   And said, "Tend that for me."
> I answered quickly, "Oh no, not that!
>   Why no one would ever see
> No matter how well my work was done,
>   Not that little place for me."
> And the words he spoke, they were not stern.
>   He answered me tenderly,
> "Ah, little one, search that heart of thine:
>   Art thou working for them or me?
> Nazareth was a little place,
>   And so was Galilee."
>
>   ("My Little Place.")

We can do it! There is not one of us who is not capable of it. Could the Father have created children who were not capable of returning to him? How could he?

I conclude my witness with an invitation to all. One of his early, great prophets put it much better than I: "And now, I would commend you to seek this Jesus of whom the prophets and apostles have written" (Ether 12:41).

May we be blessed to do so. There are those around us with knowledge and authority to help us find the way. Being one of those, I again testify "I know this man" and I love and honor him.